SOUTHERN FOOD

.... *and* ....

CIVIL RIGHTS

SOUTHERN FOOD
and
CIVIL RIGHTS

FEEDING THE REVOLUTION

Frederick Douglass Opie

AMERICAN PALATE

Published by American Palate
A Division of The History Press
Charleston, SC 29403
www.historypress.net

Copyright © 2017 by Frederick Douglass Opie
All rights reserved

First published 2017

Manufactured in the United States

ISBN 978.1.46713.738.6

Library of Congress Control Number: 2016950693

CONTENTS

Introduction   7

1. Don't Buy Where You Can't Work   9
2. Food, Jazz and Protest in Jim Crow Washington, D.C.   40
3. The "Club from Nowhere"   59
4. A Note of Support with Your Food   71
5. Where People Went to Eat, Meet, Rest, Plan and Strategize   89
6. The Sandwich Brigade   120
7. From Muslim Soup to the Famous Bean Pie   143

Afterword   155
Notes   173
Index   187
About the Author   191

INTRODUCTION

Napoleon said that an army marches on its stomach, leading to the questions: What is the relationship between food and political stability—or instability—during important periods in history? What role does food play in starting and sustaining a movement? And what important takeaways do we gain from looking at the role of food in social movements?

Southern Food and Civil Rights delves into the movements for progressive change that occurred from the 1920s through the 1960s and includes an afterword on the 2011 Occupy Wall Street movement.

The final years of completing this book on food and social movements coincided with the release of the film *The Help* and its monolithic images of African Americans as subservient, poor victims. I also completed the book while several tragic deaths of African Americans occurred in Florida, Missouri, New York, Ohio, Maryland, Louisiana and Minnesota, and in some instances, riots and movements for social justice developed thereafter. After the death of Travon Martin in Florida, I, like others, watched the subsequent emergence of the decentralized Black Lives Matter movement, for which women served as principal strategists and spokespersons. This book looks at the precursors of contemporary movements like Black Lives Matter. It shows that there have always existed movements for social justice in this country, many of them in the southern United States, where African Americans lived in their greatest concentration from the colonial period until the 1960s.[1] And food has been at the center of civil rights movements in one way or the other throughout that time.

INTRODUCTION

This book looks at the organizations and individuals, home cooks and professional chefs, who—with the food they donated, cooked, grew and distributed—helped various activists continue to march and advance their goals for progressive change and self-determination. The book also looks at movements to end discrimination in the restaurant industry for customers and would-be employees, as well as the role food has played in the Nation of Islam's economic empowerment initiatives.

Through this exploration of food and social justice, this book addresses such questions as how did African Americans view Franklin D. Roosevelt (FDR) and his National Recovery Administration (NRA) programs, particularly his job initiatives? What led to the end of Jim Crow policies in Washington, D.C. restaurants? How did progressive organizations raise the funds necessary to pay for their programs, staff and campaigns? How did striking hospital workers feed their families in New York City between 1959 in 1962? What individuals and groups made important food-related contributions to movements? How did the organizers of the March on Washington source and supply the sandwich brigade meant to provide food for the thousands of supporters who converged on the Mall in the nation's capital in 1963? Where did organizers meet and strategize in the Jim Crow South, and where did white supremacists employ violent repression against activists? Do activists have favorite restaurants? Do activists observe food rituals and traditions during strategy meetings? Oral histories and newspaper accounts provide the bulk of the primary source materials used to answer these questions.

/

DON'T BUY WHERE YOU CAN'T WORK

HISTORY OF THE MOVEMENT

In the 1920s, black newspapers informed their communities across the country about organizations dedicated to their interests. Many black neighborhoods had a local distributor of black papers that sold subscriptions to and delivered copies of the *Philadelphia Inquirer*, the *Pittsburgh Courier*, the *Chicago Tribune*, the *New Journal & Guide*, the *Afro-American* and the *New York Amsterdam News* to their customers. In most cases, African Americans in urban centers and some communities across the South could select from among several newspapers that agents offered. For example, in 1940s Tarrytown, New York, a suburb of New York City, literate African Americans subscribed to one or more of these papers and read them on a weekly basis.[2]

African American newspapers depended largely on the national black wire service, the Chicago-based Associated Negro Press, for their content. As a result, stories on new black organizations and their activities that the wire service carried quickly traveled across the country.[3]

In 1927, Chicago's Urban League chapter launched an unsuccessful campaign against the A&P grocery store company, which was refusing to hire African American clerks and managers. Two years later, the black-owned newspaper the *Chicago Whip* launched a "Don't Spend Your Money Where You Can't Work" boycott that mobilized black South Side residents in the city's Bronzeville section.[4] As local activists across the country adopted the campaign and forced white-owned companies to change their hiring practices, the direct-action strategy for engaging in progressive politics gained credibility. Furthermore, more black newspapers covered local movements, which inspired similar movements across the country.[5]

This chapter is a history of the genesis of the nonviolent direct-action movement that was the earliest of its kind and later became the distinguishing strategy of the U.S.—and largely southern—civil rights movement. These Great Depression–era movements pioneered the civil rights struggles of the 1950s and '60s, both on the streets and in courts.

The available newspaper records provide more details on some movements than others. Nonetheless, the New Negro Alliance (NNA) in Washington, D.C., had the largest and most successful direct-action movement and the one with the most detailed documentation of the 1920s through the 1940s, the decades covered in this chapter. The movement in the nation's capital included boycotts, picketing, the arrest of protesters and court cases, including the U.S. Supreme Court case *New Negro Alliance et al. v. Sanitary Grocery Co., Inc.* The March 1938 case had a profound effect on similar movements around the country and laid the foundation for future U.S. civil rights cases.[6]

THE CHICAGO MOVEMENT

In 1929, community activists James Hale Porter, lawyer and *Chicago Whip* founder and editor Joseph D. Bibb and the National Association for the Advancement of Colored People (NAACP) executive committee member and *Whip* managing editor A.C. MacNeal created the "Don't Spend Money Where You Can't Work" campaign. The movement focused on generating jobs for unemployed black workers on the South Side of Chicago.[7] Porter and MacNeal were the more militant and activist-minded, and Bibb was the even-headed legal strategist. Building on the Chicago Urban League's idea of black economic power in its campaign against the A&P and Silver Dollar Food grocery store chains, the *Whip* championed the tactic of a company boycott with daily picketing, an informational campaign and public meetings. The Urban League employed a conciliatory strategy. In contrast, the *Whip* advanced a strategy of direct confrontation. This represented the first use of direct action among black Chicago civil rights organizations. Porter convinced Bibb about the necessity of the movement, and Bibb coined the slogan "Don't Spend Money Where You Can't Work."[8]

An A&P Super Market in 1940. *Courtesy of Library of Congress.*

A labor protest in 1930. *Courtesy of Library of Congress.*

Woolworth's workers striking for a forty-hour workweek, 1937. *Courtesy of Library of Congress.*

The movement targeted the Woolworth five-and-dime stores, the only national chain in Chicago that refused to employ blacks as counter clerks in black neighborhoods. Leaders of the movement first negotiated with Woolworth to change its hiring policy without success despite the fact that African Americans accounted for 75 percent of the chain's customers in its South Side stores. Leaders of the movement called for black solidarity to break the back of one of the largest white-owned companies in the city and thereby force other white-owned companies to comply with its demands for fair hiring practices. The *Whip* maintained regular coverage of the campaign on its front pages. The leaders of the movement approached other African American newspapers about covering the campaign, but only one, the *World*, agreed. Leaders of the movement conducted the campaign in the middle of the Great Depression as a way of leveraging poor economic conditions on their behalf. Its supporters silently picketed in front of stores wearing placards covering their bodies. The picketing served as a critical element of the movement's strategy, but it began as a final resort. Picketing lasted from June 1930 until Woolworth

A grocery store in the Black Belt section of Chicago, Illinois, 1941. *Courtesy of Library of Congress.*

A storefront church and lunch wagon in the Black Belt section of Chicago, Illinois, 1941. *Courtesy of Library of Congress.*

gave in to the movement's demands in October. The original demands called for making African Americans 75 percent of the employees in African American communities in which African Americans made up 75 percent of all customers. In the end, African Americans made up 25 percent of the store's staff. The movement did, however, unite Brownsville residents, churches, civic organizations and community leaders, and it spread throughout the country.[9]

A native of Monro, Louisiana, comedian Matan Moreland became one of the first African Americans to become an A-list actor in Hollywood. Moreland married Chicago native Hazel Henry. She shared a number of his favorite recipes with Bessie M. Gant, the food writer for the Pittsburgh Courier.

MATAN MORELAND GUMBO

2 pounds okra
2 large onions
1 green pepper
3 large tomatoes
salt
pepper
bacon drippings
1 pound shrimp
2 tablespoons file powder
cooked rice, for serving

Cut okra, onions, green pepper and tomatoes fine. Put in a saucepan, add salt, pepper and bacon drippings. Cook 15 minutes, until tender. Boil shrimp in shell until tender. Peel and place in pan with other ingredients and cook for 5 minutes. Thicken with file powder. Remove and serve with rice.

Modified from the Pittsburgh Courier, *September 18, 1943*

HAZEL'S LEMON PIE

Serves 6

1 can Eagle Brand condensed milk
3 eggs, separated
3 lemons, juiced
1 box vanilla wafers
⅓ cup butter

Place condensed milk in mixing bowl. Add egg yolks and stir well. Add lemon juice and stir until thick. Combine crushed wafer and butter together carefully. Press into 9-inch pie plate. Chill until set then stand remaining wafers around sides. Pour custard into pan. Beat egg whites until stiff and place on top. Bake 10 minutes.

Modified from the Pittsburgh Courier, *September 18, 1943*

From the 1929 Chicago movement, without any national or coordinated sponsorship, movements developed in African American neighborhoods in New York City, Newark, Philadelphia, Baltimore, D.C., Richmond, Cleveland, Columbus, Toledo, Detroit, St. Louis, Los Angeles and other cities. In 1931, a successful boycott in Philadelphia against retail stores forced the retailers to open channels for hiring black workers. Similar but larger movements occurred in the nation's capital in 1933 in which the NNA's direct-action campaign resulted in an estimated $50,000 in annual payroll for newly hired African American employees.[10]

FDR'S NEW DEAL JOB PROGRAMS

The NNA consisted of young male and female graduates from northeastern colleges, most of them recent graduates serious about civic activism who were mobilized by Franklin D. Roosevelt (FDR) and his National Recovery Administration (NRA) programs, which lasted from 1933 to 1939.[11] The FDR administration viewed the NRA, in part, as a plan for the "large-scale reemployment of the idle." The legislation had a two-year term limit on it that authorized the president "to investigate labor practices, policies, wages, hours of labor, and working conditions in any trade or industry and to prescribe a limited code of fair competition, fixing maximum hours of labor, minimum rates of pay, and other working conditions."[12]

African Americans held diverse views of FDR and his NRA initiatives, including different expectations than those of the president himself about what FDR should do to provide relief for black citizens. In the tradition of Booker T. Washington and Marcus Garvey, African Americans focused on the economic independence that could be achieved as entrepreneurs or gainfully employed people. "Jobs, not relief, are the cry of the people," said a reporter in the pages of a March 1933 edition of the *Pittsburgh Courier*. "The new administration, if it would succeed, must, as quickly as possible, see to it that the dollar gets into the hands of the masses and that every man who wants to work may find a job of some kind." The article goes on to say, "The wheels of industry will begin to buzz when we have the full pocketbook and the full dinner pail in the hands of the masses in every nook and corner of the United States."[13]

From the start, organizations such as the Urban League and the NAACP lobbied for the just implementation of NRA job creation programs. The *New Journal & Guide* reported that "the Urban League, through its representatives, requested" from the administration "unprejudiced, indiscriminate consideration of" African American workers.[14] The NAACP called for African Americans to demand employment "in private industry" and encouraged unemployed African Americans in every city to organize and take the action necessary "to secure employment in businesses which obtain profits from" African Americans.[15] As one of the most progressive organizations of its time, it insisted that African Americans demand "the right of employment without discrimination" in the public and private sector as well as promoted a living wage for workers. In addition, the organization called for no agreements between the government and "organized labor, especially the American Federation of Labor (AFL) and its affiliated branches, until…such labor bodies accept African American workers as equals."[16] The NAACP encouraged black workers "to fight ceaselessly for full rights as workers" and progressive African American organizations to fight for equality for black workers as workers and citizens. It told African Americans that they should exercise their collective power as consumers to insist "that corporations and businesses which obtain profits" from blacks also employ them.[17] Progressive young African Americans' interpretations of the NRA resulted in the creation of the NNA and its militant "Buy Where You Can Work" campaign and others like it across the country.[18]

NNA'S MEMBERS AND COALITION PARTNERS

The NNA's movement focused on ending racist hiring and promoting nondiscriminatory practices in the food industry in the nation's capital. John Aubrey Davis, who had earned his undergraduate degree from Williams College and a graduate degree from the University of Wisconsin–Madison, and D.C. attorney Belford Lawson Jr. founded the organization in August 1933.[19] William H. Hastie, who graduated Phi Beta Kappa from Amherst College before earning a Harvard law degree, joined Lawson to serve as the organization's attorneys. James W. Lewis, an attorney and head of the

William H. Hastie (left) with Undersecretary of War Robert P. Patterson, 1942. *Courtesy of Library of Congress.*

commerce department of Howard University, served as the treasurer.[20] Doris Fisher and James Ward served as the co-chairs of the social committee with "one directing activities among the women and the other directing activities among the men."[21]

The organization had a two-tiered membership structure: members could pay either fifty cents or one dollar a month as membership dues for the organization. In 1933, the organization started with 300 members. By 1934, its membership campaign and successful boycotts increased its membership to 140,000. Gradually, it developed into a powerful group of African American consumers in the District of Columbia with "an auxiliary strength of nearly 1,600 supporters" from across the city.[22]

THE AFRO-AMERICAN COOKING SCHOOL (AACS)

At roughly the same time as the NNA, the Baltimore, Maryland–based *Afro-American* newspaper supported the establishment of the Afro-American Cooking School (AACS). Like the NNA, the AACS remains largely forgotten today. The sale of advertising to businesses in the food industry and kitchen appliance space underwrote the cost of admission to the school, making it free for students. Why did the paper advocate the school? Perhaps the owners of the *Afro-American* thought cooking skills would provide greater job opportunities for employment in the food industry, as domestics and small business owners. During the Great Depression, finding jobs for African Americans had been of paramount importance for the owners of the paper. The owners of the *Chicago Defender* supported a similar school. The *Afro-American* supported its cooking school on an annual basis into the late 1960s as one of its many strategies to improve career opportunities for African Americans in Baltimore and Washington, D.C.[23]

The AACS produced educational cooking materials, including exhibitions and demonstrations for African American domestic workers and housewives with the goal of improving their skills in the culinary arts. The paper viewed cooking as a marketable skill for jobseekers during the Great Depression. And cooks, caterers and restaurant owners with a slew of recipes as part of their repertoires stood greater chances of succeeding as entrepreneurs than those without. The school demonstrated and disseminated recipes to its students.[24]

Both the NNA and the AACS seem to have been inspired by Marcus Garvey's philosophy of black economics, which championed black self-

Above: A cooking demonstration in 1921. *Courtesy of the Library of Congress.*

Right: Marcus Garvey, 1924. *Courtesy of Library of Congress.*

determination through black business ownership. Jamaican-born pan-Africanist Marcus Garvey established the United Negro Improvement Association (UNIA) in Jamaica in 1914. In 1916, he moved the headquarters of the UNIA from Jamaica to Harlem in New York City. The migration of large numbers of blacks from the American South and the Caribbean basin during World War I contributed to the growth of the UNIA in North America. As a pro-business conservative, Garvey founded the Negro Factories Corporation (NFC) in 1919 and offered stock in it to African Americans as a means to help black people achieve economic independence. Among its many activities, the NFC ran grocery stores and restaurants in the early 1920s in Harlem.[25] In the 1930s and '40s, the AACS seems to have operated on a similar economic model as the UNIA. But no available sources can confirm that supposition.

In 1932, the AACS held a cooking exhibition in the Masonic Temple in Washington, D.C., that more than 4,000 people attended. African churches and fraternal organizations like the Masons provided groups like the NNA and AACS with some of the few spaces large enough to house their events in the Jim Crow South. AACS exhibitions featured free food samples for the audience and other giveaways. During the Great Depression, some audience members left the event with baskets filled with milk, flour, baking powder, ginger ale, oatmeal, boxes of corn flakes, canned beans and canned soup. Other giveaways included parcels of sweet potatoes, coffee and cakes. Sponsors also gave away from their products. The Wilkins Rogers Milling Company gave away one ton of flour, and the Try Me Bottling Company gave away five hundred bottles of soft drinks.[26] On October 7, 1933, the AACS held an exhibition at the Strand Ballroom in Baltimore. *Afro-American* coverage of the event does not mention the number of African American women who attended it. A similar event in Baltimore on October 14, 1933, attracted over 3,000 people, and a 1941 exhibition in Washington, D.C., attracted 3,300.[27]

At the AACS's Strand Ballroom exhibition, the school gave away three hundred movie tickets, one hundred baskets of food and an entire kitchen set. The gifts came from school sponsors, including the General Beverage Company, Lever Brothers Baking Company, Rumford Baking Powder Company, the Hendler Ice Cream Company, the Schmidt Baking Company, the Gunther Brewing Company, the Washington Flour Company and the Great A&P Tea Company.[28] In addition to food samples and groceries, the AACS gave away recipes, which the *Afro-American* reprinted.

AFRO COOKING SCHOOL GEORGIA COCKTAIL

1¼ cups shrimp
1 cup diced celery
1 tablespoon chopped green pepper
3 tablespoons French dressing
1 teaspoon salt
1 tablespoon lemon juice
1½ cups tomato juice

Clean shrimp and break into large pieces. Combine with celery and green pepper. Marinate in French dressing and place in a covered bowl in the refrigerator to chill. Add salt and lemon juice to the tomato juice and freeze until of a mushy consistency. Fill the bottom of cocktail glasses with two-thirds of the frozen mixture and add 2 or 3 tablespoons of the shrimp mixture. Top with remaining frozen salt, lemon and tomato juice mixture.

Modified from the Afro-American, *October 7, 1933*

AFRO COOKING SCHOOL CHEESECAKE

¼ cup butter
¾ cup sugar
5 egg yolks
2 teaspoons lemon juice
1 teaspoon grated lemon rind
1 pound cottage cheese
¾ cup flour
½ cup cream
3 egg whites

Cream butter and add sugar. When thoroughly mixed, add egg yolks, beaten separately. Add lemon juice and grated rind.

Press one pound of cheese through the potato ricer. Mix with flour and cream. Combine the two mixtures. Cut and fold in 3 egg whites, beaten stiff.

Carefully brush a spring baking dish with oil. Sprinkle inside with bread crumbs. Bake at 350 degrees Fahrenheit until firm to the touch. This will rise, settle and shrink.

Modified from the Afro-American, *November 19, 1932*

The NNA's coalition partners included thirty-five churches and civic organizations in Washington, D.C., that joined its movement and made cash contributions. The available sources do not provide detailed information on the amount attributed or on the ethnic makeup of the partners; however, it is documented that left-of-center white progressives such as the Young People's Socialist League and the Intercollegiate League for Industrial Democracy joined the NNA picket lines.[29] The NNA held meetings at an African American Masonic temple in the capital and at the YMCA on Twelfth Street in northwest Washington, D.C. Educated militant African Americans dominated the leadership positions within the NNA, which included thirteen deputy administrators, district captains and block workers with no "older Uncle Toms" among them. It created an organizational structure that would allow the "Buy Where You Can Work" campaign to reach every area of the city.[30]

The NNA adopted the Chicago movement's protest strategy almost in its entirety—its slogan ("Buy Where You Can Work"), its goal (ensuring the same opportunities for African Americans to be hired and promoted as white workers) and its tactics, negotiation and strikes (consumer boycott and picketing). But the NNA had the advantage of the passage of the NRA, FDR's dependence on African Americans for his reelection, the example of the Chicago movement, a more educated rank-and-file membership than the Chicago movement and a more sophisticated approach to analyzing its target.[31]

The Chicago movement proved that under suitable circumstances the right to strike represented African Americans' greatest weapon for achieving economic justice. It illustrated that strikes worked when the exploited population served as the economic engine of a neighborhood. Successful strikes require organization, unity, strength and "stubbornness to hold out and maintain the struggle till the end is attained," sociologist and columnist Kelly Miller said in a December 1933 article in the *New Journal & Guide*. He added that with the strike, African Americans can obtain economic justice and power and advance progressive causes.[32]

In selecting its targets, the NNA would carry out a statistical analysis of a neighborhood to determine the ratio of its African American customer base and the approximate money it spent to the number of blacks the store employed and their positions. Next, an NNA committee would petition a targeted company to hire and/or promote African American employees based on the survey results. The NNA would boycott and picket companies that did not comply with its demands.[33]

NNA CAMPAIGNS

Temple Luncheonette and Drug Company Campaign

After the NNA's establishment in August 1933, a U Street hamburger grill became its first target for ending racist hiring practices and working conditions in the District. Using a boycott, the NNA swiftly pressured company officials to rehire two fired black employees. (Unfortunately, additional records on the campaign could not be found.)[34] Around Labor Day, the NNA started analyzing the Temple Luncheonette and Drug Company that operated near the Masonic temple at Tenth and U Streets, an African American neighborhood in northwest Washington, D.C. Owner Louis Hurwitz had promised African American waitresses at his establishment "$14.50 a week provided they would turn over their tips to the management."[35] When they refused, Hurwitz reduced their salary to $3.00 a week, from which he deducted the cost of their meals, which he required them to eat on the job, and the cost of "the laundering of their uniforms," leading to debt peonage for some.[36] Based on its investigation and statistical analysis, the NNA sent Hurwitz a registered letter requesting a meeting to discuss working conditions, hiring practices, wages, working hours and promotions. Following a series of negotiations in September between the NNA and Hurwitz, the NNA gave a ten-day warning to comply with its demands for more equitable hiring practices, working conditions and promotion opportunities.[37] When Hurwitz failed to comply, the NNA launched a boycott about mid-September against the Temple Luncheonette and Drug Company that forced Hurwitz to renegotiate. After further talks before the end of September, the company agreed to hire an African American chief dietitian and general manager, provide all employees with a meal per day and pay waitresses on a commission basis plus 10 percent of their gross sales. The company also agreed to give Howard University students majoring in finance first consideration for related job openings in the company.[38]

The A&P Campaign

Once the NAA concluded its Temple Luncheonette and Drug Company campaign, it began an analysis of the A&P grocery store chain in African American neighborhoods in northwest Washington, D.C. Its analysis concluded that the company had unequal hiring and promotion practices.

The exterior of a grocery store, 1942. *Courtesy of Library of Congress.*

The interior of a grocery store, 1920. *Courtesy of Library of Congress.*

The interior of a grocery store, 1937. *Courtesy of Library of Congress.*

In mid-September 1933, the NNA sent A&P officials a letter demanding that they hire African American clerks in the Ninth and S Street Northwest store. About a week later, it then followed up with a letter stating that it had waited a reasonable length of time for a reply to the demand. Company officials ignored the coalition.[39] At a September 23 meeting, the NNA began planning a boycott of the store. Two days later, "hundreds of people gathered as several young men carrying sandwich signs began their patrol of the A&P store at [Ninth] and S Streets, telling prospective buyers, 'Do Your Part, Buy Where You Can Work; No Negroes Employed Here.'"[40] Many African Americans who came to shop did not enter the store after they read the signs. By noon, sales dropped sharply. The NNA continued to picket A&P stores into October.

Meanwhile, the NNA began analyzing and targeting the Sanitary Grocery Company and Piggly Wiggly food stores. It sent out a call urging all African American customers to take their business elsewhere until A&P officials met their demands to hire black clerks in its stores in black communities. Later a similar boycott call went to protest the Piggly Wiggly's policies. The NNA also organized informational speaking engagements across the city to raise support for its work.[41] D.C. police arrested the NNA's Dutton Ferguson and James Ward on the charge of violating "a new sign regulation, which prescribed that signs for advertising purposes must not exceed a certain size, and persons displaying such signs must have a police permit."[42] The presiding judge for the case, Gus A. Schuldt, dismissed the charges but not before praising the brief that NNA attorneys Hastie and Lawson submitted to the court. Hastie would later represent the NNA in the 1938 U.S. Supreme Court case *New Negro Alliance et al. v. Sanitary Grocery Co., Inc.*[43]

Reports of a similar movement came out of Columbus and Toledo, Ohio. Reverend W. Payne Stanley, pastor of All Saints Episcopal Church in Toledo, served as president of the Toledo branch of the NAACP. He led successful boycotts against the Kroger grocery and baking company chain.[44] The *Cleveland Call* (also at times called the *Cleveland Call & Post*) was an important African American–operated newspaper that served Ohio's sizable population of African Americans from the South, as well as covered stories from around the country. The paper, like others of its time, had a food section with recipes reflective of a readership with roots in the Mississippi Delta and Louisiana. The following recipes are a case in point.

CHICKEN GUMBO

Serves 4

1 medium-size (3-pound) chicken, cut into serving pieces
salt and pepper
flour, for dredging
salt pork, for frying
1 onion, finely chopped
½ red pepper, finely chopped
4 cups okra, cooked
1 sprig parsley
1½ cups tomato paste
3 cups boiling water
herbs to taste, file and bay leaf recommended
1 cup cooked rice

Sprinkle chicken with salt and pepper and dredge with flour. Render salt pork and sauté chicken until tender. Fry onion in fat left in pan—add red pepper, okra and parsley. Cook slowly for 10 to 15 minutes. Add tomato paste, water and 1½ teaspoons of salt and whatever other herbs you desire. Cook slowly until chicken is tender. Serve with cooked rice.

Modified from the Cleveland Call & Post, May 20, 1950

SHRIMP JAMBALAYA

Serves 4 generously

1 cup raw rice
salt
1 slice tenderized ham
½ pound hot link sausage*
1 large onion, diced
½ cup diced celery
1 green pepper, chopped
1 pound cooked shrimp
1 tablespoon chopped parsley
1 teaspoon thyme
1 bay leaf
½ teaspoon cayenne pepper
1 small can tomato paste
¼ cup water

If hot link sausage is not available, increase cayenne pepper measure to ¾ teaspoon

Boil rice for 25 minutes in salted water in a large vessel; when done, blanch rice with cold water and drain. While rice is boiling, prepare other ingredients as follows. Dice ham and fry for several minutes. Then remove from pan. Fry sausage in onion, celery and green pepper, but do not brown them. Add ham, sausage, shrimp, seasonings, tomato paste, water and rice. Cook thoroughly for 5 minutes more.

Modified from the Cleveland Call & Post, *May 20, 1950*

Back in the nation's capital, the A&P strike continued into December 1933. During the initial talks, A&P agreed to hire African American clerks in five stores but refused to move beyond using the majority of its black employees as janitors, a position that paid less than clerks. The NNA pushed the company to hire an entire African American staff, including managers, in stores that depended on African American patronage for their success.[45] About a week before Christmas, the NNA turned up the pressure on A&P, placing protesters in front of thirteen additional A&P stores. The tactic worked, forcing company officials into negotiation with the NNA. The boycott resulted in A&P officials hiring an entire clerical staff of African Americans at stores located on Seventh,

Ninth, Eleventh, Fourteenth and Eighteenth Streets in northwest Washington, D.C. The A&P superintendent of stores in the District explained that the new hires made good sense from a business standpoint because it increased sales "volume for the company and would not be looked upon as charity."[46] He added that within a year, the company's African American employees would have the same opportunity for advancement and promotion as any other employee of the company and that within a year, African American residents in the District could look forward to the development of black managers in each of the stores where black clerks had started working. "Worthy [black] clerks" would be able to get a promotion to manager following a one-year training program.[47] Following the boycott, the NNA started doing research on "borderline" stores that straddled black and white neighborhoods as part of its next campaign.[48]

High's Ice Cream Store Campaign

The NAA ended its boycott against A&P and turned its attention to L.W. High and his twenty-six High's Ice Cream stores, the majority of which were located in predominantly African American neighborhoods. The company refused to respond to the NAA's request for it to hire African American clerks. NNA's Henry Anderson supervised the boycott against High's. He told a reporter, "This is a tough job, but we are prepared to camp here for the next six months to get results. Our enthusiasm grows as these hard-boiled employers take their time about coming to terms."[49] In August 1934, the NNA began its High's boycott at the company's store on Eleventh Street. A *New Journal & Guide* reporter assessed the situation after being on the scene for four consecutive days, writing, "I have on no other occasion seen colored people rally to a cause with so much enthusiasm before. I am becoming more converted every day to the theory—that there is a New Negro."[50]

In response to the boycott, High's filed a suit against the NNA in D.C. courts. The dispute went all the way to the D.C. Supreme Court. High's claimed the picketing of its store interfered with the operation of his business. The NNA argued that it had the right to protest against the company's discriminatory hiring practices, adding that the company's Eleventh Street store operated in a community where 70 percent of the residents were African Americans and, therefore, the company had the responsibility to hire African American clerks. The judge ordered the NNA to cease all picketing until the court rendered a decision. NNA's attorneys Hastie and Lawson successfully filed a motion for an appeal of the injunction.

Above: A soda jerk flips ice cream into a malted milk shake in 1939. *Courtesy of Library of Congress.*

Right: A soda jerk passes ice cream soda in 1936. *Courtesy of Library of Congress.*

AFRO COOKING SCHOOL VANILLA ICE CREAM

3 tablespoons minute tapioca
2 cups milk
¼ teaspoon salt
⅓ cup sugar, plus 2 tablespoons
3 tablespoons light corn syrup
2 egg whites
1 cup cream, whipped
1 tablespoon vanilla

Add minute tapioca to milk and cook in double boiler for 15 minutes, or until tapioca is clear and mixture thickened, stirring constantly. Strain hot mixture, stirring (not rubbing) through sieve into a bowl with salt, ⅓ cup sugar and corn syrup. Stir until sugar is dissolved. Cool. Add 2 tablespoons sugar to egg whites and beat until stiff. Fold into cream and add vanilla. Turn into freezing tray of refrigerator and freeze as rapidly as possible. Usually 3 to 4 hours required.

Modified from the Afro-American, *November 19, 1932*

ORANGE SHERBET

1 teaspoon granulated gelatin
½ cup cold water
1½ cups sugar
1½ cups boiling water
grated rind of two oranges
1½ cups orange juice
1 cup lemon juice
1 pint heavy cream
½ cup sugar
pinch salt
2 eggs

Soak gelatin in cold water for about 5 minutes. Dissolve gelatin and sugar in boiling water. Add orange rind and orange and lemon juices. Turn into freezing tray and freeze to a mush, stirring once during freezing. Beat cream to custard consistency and add sugar and salt. Separate yolks from whites of the eggs. Beat yolks until thick and lemon colored and whites until stiff. Add to cream. Combine with frozen mixture and continue the freezing, stirring twice more during the process.

Modified from the Chicago Defender, *October 26, 1935*

Sweet Potato Ice Cream

½ cup sugar
1 cup boiled, mashed and strained sweet potatoes
1 egg white
1 cup cream, beaten well

Add sugar to mashed boiled sweet potatoes. Beat egg white until stiff and add to the sweet potato mixture. Put in ordinary freezer. When it begins to freeze add well-beaten cream.

This may be flavored as desired and varied by using some brown sugar.

Modified from the Atlanta Daily World, *June 30, 1934*

This was the second time in the organization's history in which its opponent filed an injunction against its picketing and its legal team appealed a D.C. court decision. Kaufmann's department store had also filed suit against the NNA boycott of its store on Seventh Street in northwest Washington, D.C. Jacob and Isaac Kaufmann founded the department store company in Pittsburgh in 1871 as a men's store on the South Side. They built the original flagship store in downtown Pittsburgh in 1887. The company operated stores in the Northeast until 1946, when the May Company Department Stores of California purchased it. In December 1933, the NNA had petitioned a Kaufmann's department store in the nation's capital to hire African Americans as part of its sales force (particularly behind store counters) and allow employees to work together side by side regardless of their complexion. After the start of the "perfectly timed" Kaufmann's boycott (just before Christmas), store sales had dwindled by one-third. Kaufmann attorneys called NNA picketers in front of the store "a public nuisance" and a violation of the Norris-LaGuardia Act, a law Congress passed in 1932 that outlawed picketing during labor disputes.[51]

The District of Columbia court imposed an injunction against the NNA on December 20, 1933, with Kaufman attorneys arguing that the NNA violated the Norris-LaGuardia Act. No sooner had the injunction been issued than the Young People's Socialist League, an organization with an all-white membership, mobilized to picket the store for the sidelined NNA members. League members who took up the picketing included Robert Shosteck, a George Washington University student and secretary of the local branch of the league; Roland Parris, a graduate of Washington State College; Joel Seidman and M.P. Pogey of Johns Hopkins University; Monroe Sweetland, a graduate of Syracuse University; Joseph Zamere of a Los Angeles junior college; and Martha Nusbaum, secretary of the Young People's Socialist league. Shosteck said that immediately after learning about the injunction against the NNA he spent several hours telephoning in an effort to get picketers in front of the store. On December 22, 1933, the courts modified the injunction, adding the league to the original December 20, 1933 injunction.[52] At the end of January 1934, NNA attorneys Belford V. Lawson, Thelma D. Ackis and William H. Hastie filed a formal motion of appeal to end the temporary injunction against the organization. The NNA legal team based its appeal on the Norris-LaGuardia Act, insisting it engaged in fighting race-based discrimination in hiring and promotion practices on the job.[53]

The organization used the injunction to organize a membership campaign. "Our membership campaign is designed to reinforce and completely build our organization into a powerful weapon with which and through which every neighbor in the city will benefit from our buy-where-you-can-work program," said the NNA's Albert Desmond. (His position in the organization is unclear.)[54] In December 1936, almost a year later, the Kaufmann case remained pending with the injunction still in place.

After the Kaufmann injunction, other targets of NNA boycotts and picketing, including the High Ice Cream Company and then the Sanitary Grocery Company, would go on to file similar injunctions against the picket-carrying progressive protest organization. NNA legal counsel would spend several years fighting the anti-picketing injunctions through the court of appeals, arguing in favor of the right to protest against discrimination in hiring practices and promotions. The court battle made its way to the U.S. Supreme Court in 1938. On picket lines in front of luncheonettes, grocery stores, department stores, ice cream stores and in the courts, the NNA had become engaged in a national struggle for "economic justice for the working people of America," said Desmond.[55]

New Negro Alliance et al. v. Sanitary Grocery Co., Inc.

In 1936, the Sanitary Grocery Company, which included Piggly Wiggly grocery stores, operated 255 grocery, meat and vegetable stores; a warehouse; and a bakery in the District of Columbia. The company employed white and black workers but had no black clerks or managers. In April, the company opened a new store at 1936 Eleventh Street Northwest in a predominantly African American neighborhood. The NNA sent out its usual first tactical approach and requested that the company hire blacks as clerks and managers, particularly in stores African American customers patronized. The company refused, so the NNA launched a boycott of the Eleventh Street and other company stores. The Sanitary Grocery Company filed suit with the D.C. District Court, claiming that the NNA engaged in activities that prevented the proper conduct and operation of its business. A D.C. judge ordered the NNA to cease "from picketing or patrolling" all company stores and "boycotting or urging others to boycott" the stores.[56] Hastie again represented the NNA before the D.C. Court of Appeals, which upheld the injunction. He then appealed to the U.S. Supreme Court, which agreed to hear the case in March 1938. The court heard both sides present on March 2 and 3, convened and rendered a decision on March 28. In a 6–2 decision, the court decided in favor of the NNA, declaring it lawful to boycott "terms and conditions of employment in an industry or a plant or a place of business" should it choose to do.[57] Until 1938, the courts remained opposed to civil rights or labor organizations using boycott as a civil rights strategy. The decision inspired organizations across the country to utilize the boycott in their struggles for equal opportunities for black workers.[58]

THE MOVEMENT SPREADS

The Urban League took the lead in mobilizing African American residents in St. Louis. The civil rights organization led a similar movement against white-owned chain stores in a forty-five-block business community in the city's black neighborhood. The movement "met unusual success in forcing small neighborhood stores to employ [African Americans]," reported the *Cleveland Call & Post*. "In one instance, a chain store [unnamed] refused to negotiate with one of the groups." The members organized a boycott and "almost immediately its sales dropped to only a few dollars a day," forcing management to the negotiation table.[59] Another group, called the Colored Clerks Circle and composed of high school and college graduates, organized a successful boycott against the unnamed chain store company and independent stores "that resulted in the hiring of 240 clerks."[60] The Communist Party in Los Angeles organized a successful boycott against the Kress 5-10-25 Cent Stores for its refusal to hire black workers. The campaign later expanded to other unnamed stories in the city.[61]

In October 1938, the African American labor leader A. Philip Randolph, president of the Brotherhood of Sleeping Car Porters, charged that while the American Federation of Labor (AFL) itself did not discriminate, twenty of its national and international affiliates did. African Americans had to fight for jobs and a place in trade unions.[62] Toward that effort, sixty black organizations "representing 150,000 milk users in Chicago" staged a "milkless day" strike in October in protest of the milk delivery company that refused to hire African American drivers and the union that represented the white drivers that delivered the milk.[63]

In the Midwest, Local 136 of the United Bakery and Food Handlers in Michigan went on strike against Kroger in support of the movement in Ohio demanding that the company hire qualified black managers. The union also demanded that black employees of the company receive the same wages as white workers. Historically, Kroger had refused to hire black workers as store managers, even in black neighborhoods, and restricted black employees to menial jobs at much lower pay than white workers performing the same tasks. Championing the stand taken by the union, the Detroit Council of the NNC and other organizations "joined in vigorous protests against police attacks on the picket lines in homes of the strikers," reported the *Call & Post*.[64] In the winter of 1939, the Harlem-based Coordinating Committee for Employment (CCE) organized a campaign against the AFL and the Congress of Industrial Organizations (CIO) in protest of white union locals who refused blacks as members and prevented them from being hired as drivers on milk, bread and beer trucks.[65]

The Reverend Adam Clayton Powell Jr. of the Harlem-based Abyssinian Baptist Church served as the CCE's leader years before he ran for public office. The CCE included Garveyites, migrants from the U.S. South and the Caribbean and some leftists. The group met at Powell's church, which had a membership of ten thousand.[66] By 1940, Harlem had more progressive organizations involved in direct action "than any other city in the world, each designed as a panacea for any ill," wrote a reporter in the pages of the *Call & Post*. The Negro Industrial and Clerical Alliance took up pickets against stores in Harlem that refused to hire African Americans or did so only as part of the janitorial staff and never as clerks. "Out of this movement grew the Citizens' League for Fair Play," which gained the endorsement and support of "sixty-two organizations, including eighteen leading churches," reported the *Call & Post*. The Citizens' League for Fair Play picketed stores on 125th Street in Harlem, leading some to start hiring black store clerks.[67]

The movement in Harlem operated similarly to the movements in Chicago and Washington, D.C., in terms of its slogan and strategy. In Harlem, a CCE boycott forced the Chock Full o' Nuts Restaurant chain to start employing African Americans. The Uptown Chamber of Commerce negotiated with the CCE and signed a binding agreement ending employment discrimination among its members.[68] In November 1940, three thousand people attended a CCE mass meeting at Powell's church, during which CCE leader Ellis A. Williams called for organizing a campaign against General Foods, best described as one of the largest food production companies and employers in the Northeast.[69] The documented history, unfortunately, provides no indication of the company's hiring practices or if the CCE went forward with the boycott.

The *New York Amsterdam News* food writer Ann Schuyler, most likely a southerner, had this to say about the southern cook and sweet potato recipes:

> [W]e don't have just one or two ways of cooking these succulent tubers. We use them candied, and delicate soufflés that quiver as they come to the table, combined with apples,

*and in pies that for sheer flavor leave the pumpkin pie of
New Englanders in the background. They go into biscuits
and into—pone but it would be impossible to list the many
uses to which we put them. Suffice to say that each is better
than the last and it's purely a question of individual taste
which one prefers....To descend from the poetry of flavor
the prose of dollars and cents, you find the sweet potato
recommending itself from the point of view of economy
too. Sweet potatoes 558 calories per pound against 378 in
white potatoes. And of course the sugar we use in cooking
them is a concentrated fuel food which adds to their food
value as well as their goodness. Taken together it would be
hard to beat sugar and sweet potatoes as a source of body
heat and energy at low cost.*[70]

CANDIED SWEET POTATOES

boiled sweet potatoes
butter
sugar
cinnamon

Cut boiled sweet potatoes into long slices. Place in an earthen
dish; put ¼ teaspoon butter on each slice; sprinkle well with
sugar. Pour in sufficient water to cover the bottom of the dish.
Dust lightly with cinnamon. Bake until the sugar and butter
have candied and the potatoes are brown.

Modified from the New York Amsterdam News, *August 13, 1930*

Ollie Stewart was born 1906 in Gibsland, Louisiana. He
graduated in 1930 from what is now Tennessee State University
in Nashville, Tennessee, and thereafter began submitting
freelance articles to notable publications. He gained acclaim
for an article he did on Father Divine called "Harlem's God
in His Heaven" that was published in *Reader's Digest*, for which
he received $650, a large sum in 1940. The *Afro-American* hired

him as the paper's New York correspondent. He provided a vivid description of the food scene in Harlem in 1941. On the avenues you could see eye candy of all kinds. From the food of street vendors to the windows of restaurants and delicatessens, you could find whole roasting chickens or a "yard of spareribs turning magically on the spit," he wrote. On the side streets you would be bombarded with the delicious "aromas of buttered biscuits, candied sweets, and rice baptized in sausage gravy." At hole-in-the-wall basement eateries "gourmands stuff themselves" on pot licker, pig's feet, chitterlings and corn pone.

The culinary variety that existed in Harlem of the 1940s: Jamaican curry dishes, Puerto Rican arroz con pollo (tender meat of chicken smothered in rice), black beans and fried plantains garnished with slices of avocado. Harlem had a restaurant that specialized in the cuisine of New Orleans with such dishes as shrimp gumbo with okra, crawfish bisque and jambalaya. The cook from Jacksonville did fried mullet served with hominy and greens. You could find Tidewater restaurants with Virginia puddings and barbecue and hot tamale restaurants that made Texas plates. Visit the Maryland joint to find fried chicken and beaten biscuits, the Alabama restaurant for great cornbread and the Tennessee joint for moonshine. "It's all in Harlem, and it's advertised by huge signs. You just take your pick," said Stewart. In 1940s Harlem, a barbecue trend broke out in which large crowds waited in line at places such as Chef Otis of Bon Go on St. Nicholas Avenue for famous barbecued meats.[71]

CHEF OTIS'S OLD-FASHIONED BARBECUE SAUCE

2 small cans tomato paste
1 tablespoon Worcestershire sauce
1 lemon, juiced
1 cup vinegar
½ cup French mustard
1 tablespoon salt
1 teaspoon black pepper

1 tablespoon crushed pepper
2 garlic cloves
1 pint beef broth
1 pint water

Mix all ingredients well. Cook for 35 minutes. Strain and serve hot over meat.

Modified from the Afro-American, *May 3, 1941*

CHEF OTIS'S BASTING MOP SAUCE

For 10 pounds of ribs or basting while meat is cooking and also before it is put over the fire.
8 ounces ketchup
2 cups vinegar
2 tablespoons Worcestershire sauce
1 cup French mustard
1 tablespoon each salt and black pepper

Mix together all ingredients and use to as you cook the meat. Baste the meat with a mop (people used new, stringy cloth mobs to apply the basting sauce to barbecuing meat) every 15 minutes. Cooked over a hot coal fire. It should be done in 45 minutes. Serve meat with old-fashioned sauce.

Modifed from the Afro-American, *May 3, 1941*

CONCLUSION

Starting with the 1929 "Don't Spend Money Where You Can't Work" Chicago movement, without any national or coordinated sponsorship, movements developed across black neighborhoods in urban North America. As discussed in the opening of this chapter, before the civil rights and black power movements, African American newspapers depended on the national black wire service as their primary news source, and stories on new black organizations and their activities traveled across the country via weekly black-owned periodicals. Through black newspapers, the 1929 direct-action movement that started in Chicago made its way across the country. African American organizations experimented with it in battles for jobs in and around the food industry. They made adjustments to the direct-action strategy based on local conditions. It proved successful in many black neighborhoods seeking economic justice.

In 1934, NNA co-founder Davis would go on to work as a research assistant to Lieutenant Lawrence A. Oxley, chief of the Division of Negro Labor in the U.S. Department of Labor under FDR. Oxley served as one of FDR's so-called black cabinet members. FDR appointed NNA attorney William Hastie assistant solicitor for the U.S. Department of the Interior. It seems plausible that these appointments represented the administration's attempt to dismantle the NNA and stop its successful direct-action movement in the nation's capital, as well as cease its inspiration of similar movements around the country. These movements from 1927 to 1940 gave the buying-power and direct-action strategies for engaging in progressive politics credibility. They proved so effective that civil rights strategists and organizations of the 1950s and 1960s added them to their toolboxes and employed them across the country.

FOOD, JAZZ AND PROTEST IN JIM CROW WASHINGTON, D.C.

WASHINGTON, D.C. EATERIES

In the 1940s through the early 1960s, Washington, D.C., had predominantly Jim Crow restaurants and cafeterias that catered to a "whites only" customer base. Historically, U.S. officials created the nation's capital out of the southern territories of Virginia and Maryland, and a small but powerful block of Dixiecrats ensured that Jim Crow kept eateries in the city segregated. Those who lived and worked in D.C. also had to endure the "battle of the plate," referring to the long lines outside restaurants with high customer demand but inferior food and service. African Americans found few places to eat in and around the capital and, as a result, walked blocks past segregated restaurants and cafeterias in order to get a meal. A number of government buildings with cafeterias, including the Department of Justice cafeteria and the Federal Reserve Bank building cafeteria, refused to serve African Americans. Operators of "standup counters" serving hot dogs, hamburgers, cold drinks and pies, along with five-and-dime stores downtown, also did not welcome African American customers. Some lunch counters at downtown department stores catered to black customers, but the same stores would not serve African Americans in their tearooms, which served light meals, appetizers and sandwiches. African Americans could, however, obtain a meal at some restaurants and cafeterias.[72] This chapter focuses on Washington, D.C.—the segregated eateries, the battle over home rule and the civil rights movement—through the lens of food.

The renowned artist and native southerner Dr. David C. Driskell arrived in Washington, D.C., in 1949 to attend Howard University as an undergraduate. He was born in 1931 in Eatonton, Georgia, into a family of farmers and grew up in the Foote Hill Blue Ridge region of the Appalachian Mountains in Rutherford County, North Carolina. After he graduated in 1955, he returned to the capital to enter Catholic University's masters of fine arts program in 1958.[73] Catholic University was one of the few schools "considered in the South that had accepted blacks into the graduate school programs....I don't know from the founding, but certainly in the twentieth century." He lived with his sister at 309 A Street Northeast in a prestigious black community of "domestics and people who worked day jobs." They were middle-class African Americans who lived and ate well in homes three blocks behind the U.S. Supreme Court Building.[74]

SWEET POTATO PIE

A good pie which definitely dispenses with the hungry feelings, is
easy to prepare...and also very appetizing is a sweet potato pie.
—*Chicago Defender*, August 19, 1939

The real test of any kind of pie is not the filling but the crust....
Flaky light pastry is possible when the housewife uses measured
amounts of flour and shortening with just the right amount of
water to hold the dough together. Too much handling develops
a tough crust so add water slowly, mix gently, and roll lightly.
—*New Journal & Guide*, December 18, 1937.[75]

Makes 9-inch pie

¾ cup sugar
¼ teaspoon salt
¾ teaspoon ground cinnamon
½ teaspoon ground nutmeg
¼ teaspoon ground ginger
¼ teaspoon ground allspice
¼ cup cooked and mashed sweet potatoes
3 eggs

1¼ cups milk
3 tablespoons orange juice
¾ teaspoon grated orange rind
¼ cup butter, melted and cooled

Mix sugar, salt and spices. Add to sweet potatoes. Beat in eggs, milk, orange juice, grated orange rind and butter. Pour into unbaked pastry shell and bake in hot oven (400 degrees Fahrenheit) for 10 minutes. Reduce heat to moderate (350 degrees Fahrenheit) and finish baking.

Modified from the New Journal & Guide, *December 18, 1937*

As a student, Driskell ate most of his meals at his sister's house. His sister was "an excellent cook….I remember her sweet potato pie." He noted, "You could not eat out at just any place" because of Jim Crow laws, so restaurants that catered to "coloreds" flourished due to segregation that restricted the public dining options for African Americans.[76] In northwest D.C., you could find good food at black-owned restaurants in the old U Street Northwest corridor, now called the Shaw neighborhood. During the first half of the twentieth century, it became a jazz haven for Washingtonians with various clubs, such as Crystal Caverns (later renamed Bohemian Cavern), Lincoln Colonnade, Club Bengasi, Gypsy West, the Hotel Cario ballroom, Northeast Casino and Club Prudhom, among others. These venues propelled local music careers and hosted legendary jazz artists, including Louis Amstrong. The U Street corridor can best be described as a stop on the famed "Chitlin' Circuit," a string of black-owned and operated honky-tonks, nightclubs and more elaborate theaters that stretched from Nashville to New York. Entertainers called it the Chitlin' Circuit because some club owners sold iconic soul food dishes, including pickled pigs' feet and chitlins. Other nearby eateries opened and did the same. The U Street section had a number of these smaller nightclubs and bar and grills that featured jazz music and food. These establishments catered to black customers in search of soulful jazz music and food.[77]

A typical menu in a Washington jazz club and restaurant in the 1940s and '50s included "barbecued pork, lima beans, rice, sweet potatoes, Hominy grits, mashed potatoes, green peas," and, surprisingly, "spaghetti."[78] The Lunford

Louis Armstrong All-Stars perform in Club Bali at 1901 Fourteenth Street Northwest in 1947. *Courtesy of the Historical Society of Washington, D.C.*

The dining room of the Whitelaw Hotel, 1839 Thirteenth and T Streets, circa 1929. *Courtesy of the Historical Society of Washington, D.C.*

The kitchen of the Whitelaw Hotel, circa 1929. *Courtesy of the Historical Society of Washington, D.C.*

Beer Garden and Restaurant ran a newspaper ad that said: "Still offering that special half-fried chicken dinner with 2 vegetables for $.35 daily!" The owner, R.V. Lunford, noted that his restaurant, located at 1620 U Street Northwest, featured "that good old home cooking" and that it represented "one of the best places to get really good food and ice cold beer."[79] Anna Jean Clore owned and operated Clore's Guest House, which gained a national reputation as "a headquarters for good food" in the nation's capital.

BARBECUED SPARERIBS

"To say that barbecue is a favorite food in the South is to be guilty of serious understatement. To say that barbecue not only is a food, but a part of the tradition of the South, comes near the truth. We Southerners take our barbecue hot or cold, highly seasoned or not so much and we take it all year round," reported the July 19, 1940 *Atlanta Constitution.*

---

4 pounds spareribs
2 tablespoons fat
2 tablespoons butter or margarine
1 medium onion, finely chopped
2 tablespoons vinegar
2 tablespoons brown sugar
4 tablespoons lemon juice
1 to 3 tablespoons cayenne pepper
1 cup ketchup
3 tablespoons Worcestershire sauce
1 to 2 teaspoons ground mustard
1 cup water
1 to 2 cups chopped celery, or 1 tablespoon celery salt
3 or 4 potatoes (for serving)

Brown the spareribs on both sides in the hot fat. Remove to a baking pan. Melt butter or margarine and brown the onions in it. Add remaining ingredients, except the potatoes. When very hot pour over the spare ribs. Place baking pan containing spare ribs in a 350-degree oven and bake about 1½ hours. Baked potatoes to serve with these ribs may be cooked in the oven along with the ribs. Wash potatoes, rub with a little cooking fat and lay them on the rack in the oven. The slow heat, which is right for the baking ribs, is right, too, for the potatoes. Baked potatoes always should be baked in a slow or moderately slow oven for best results.

Modified from the Atlanta Constitution, *July 19, 1940*

VIRGINIA FRIED CHICKEN WITH FRIED MUSH AND CREAM GRAVY

2 frying chickens
3 cups boiling water
1 teaspoon salt, plus additional
1 cup white cornmeal
1 egg yolk
½ flour, plus 1 tablespoon

lard
1 tablespoon butter
1 cup thin cream

Disjoint and wash the chickens. Bring the water and salt to a full boil and then sift in the cornmeal slowly to prevent lumping. Cook for 30 minutes over low heat. Then cool and add the egg yolk. Dredge the chicken with ½ flour and salt, and then brown in hot lard (the fat should be ½-inch deep in heavy frying pan). Brown each piece slowly. Then drain on absorbent paper and set aside in a warm place. Into the same frying pan, drop spoonsfuls of the mush to form thin, round cakes. Brown on each side and arrange in a border around the chicken. Add the butter to the same frying pan, blend with 1 tablespoon flour and then add the cream. Stir until slightly thickened, season with salt and pepper and serve with the fried chicken and mush.

Modified from the China Press, *September 11, 1936*

LIMAS WITH SAUSAGE

1 medium-size onion, diced
½ pound sausage
1 cup cooked or dried limas
1 cup tomatoes
½ teaspoon chili
½ teaspoon salt

Fry onions and sausage until well done. Add other ingredients and simmer for 30 minutes.

Modified from the Philadelphia Tribune, *October 8, 1936*

Similarly, Lloyd V. Blaine earned a reputation for good food. He had worked at the popular Just Barbecue 1 and 2 in the city before opening "the swank Club Bengasi."[80] In the 1950s, the club featured prominent jazz artists, such as the brilliant saxophonist Lester Young, and its menu had "more than 30 tempting salads and meats that put home cooking to shame."[81] Clubs like the Bohemian Cavern on Eleventh Street Northwest had "hosted virtually every famous jazz musician—from Charlie Parker to Thelonious Monk—who ever passed through the town," and they had good food.[82]

The menus represented a continuum of the cookery that came from the slave quarters and special-occasion meals during the antebellum period. After the end of slavery, they first became part of the menus of rural makeshift juke joints. Later, you could find them in the urban night clubs and bar and grills where working-class blacks gathered to collectively relax and recover from the stress of Jim Crow. Also in violation of Jim Crow laws and customs, some white men became regulars to these black working-class leisure spaces.

In the meantime, the District Employment Center in the Capitol refused to hire African American men for all types of restaurant work, yet white-controlled newspapers and politicians criticized these men for not having jobs and being on public relief.

Three Integrated Eateries in D.C.

There were, however, three exceptions in the District where black and white professionals could enjoy good food in an integrated atmosphere: the Saverin Restaurant at Union Station; a restaurant in the building that served as the national headquarters for the Methodist Church, located across the street from the House of Representatives on North Capitol Street, right next to the Supreme Court building; and a cafeteria in the National Gallery of Art. With the exception of David Driskell's oral history, gaps exist in sources and information on the restaurants, particularly related to their recipes and photos.

The Saverin Restaurant at Union Station was part of a larger restaurant chain with locations in the District and into the New England region. David Driskell recalled that "as late as the 1960s, it was still operating on I-95 in New York in places like that." He described it as a lavish "concession restaurant" that was "like a diner but [with] better food than a diner."[83] It was similar to the Sanborns chain in Mexico. Available sources do not provide insight as to why the Saverin did not discriminate.

The cafeteria in the headquarters of the United Methodist Church had "wonderful" food, recalled Driskell, "but if you weren't a professor or a high-class minister you didn't know about it." One of his professors from

Howard "who loved good food" took him there. "He was an excellent cook himself and taught me and my wife a lot about cooking."[84]

The cafeteria in the National Gallery of Art was another place where black professionals ate good food in an integrated setting. Banker, industrialist, philanthropist and art collector Andrew W. Mellon donated the majority of the funding for the gallery. As a progressive southerner, Mellon mandated that "the facility had to be open to everybody," and "he had a policy that anyone could eat there [and it had] good food…delightful cooking," said Driskell."[85]

In short, if you wanted good food in an integrated place, you could go to the Saverin Restaurant at Union Station, the cafeteria in the headquarters of the United Methodist Church or a cafeteria in the National Gallery of Art—"those three places," said Driskell.[86]

Like most African Americans of his generation, Driskell did not like how Jim Crow policies in the capital limited his restaurant choices. He and others like him negotiated and resisted these and other such policies in their daily business.

Segregated Eateries in Washington, D.C.

In the mid-twentieth century, our nation's capital was setting a horrible example for the rest of the country with segregated restaurants. In December 1948, the National Committee on Segregation in the nation's capital disclosed that segregation and eating places in D.C. had no legal foundation.

During a brief period when the district held the power of home rule, from 1872 to 1873, it passed a statute prohibiting discrimination in restaurants in Washington, D.C., under an 1872 civil rights law. The laws prohibited restaurants, hotels, barbershops and other public facilities from refusing service to anyone because of race. A similar law passed in 1873 took most of the business out of the 1872 law, but restaurants remained. A 1901 district code drawn up after the end of home rule dropped this law from the statute books. The 1873 law had still been in effect and enforced until 1912, even after Congress recodified district legislation in 1901.[87]

Thirty-seven D.C. community organizations and concerned citizens and activists studying antidiscrimination laws in the nation's capital formed a group called the Coordinating Committee for the Enforcement of D.C. Anti-Discrimination Laws (CCEDA). In 1948, this group uncovered the disappearance of the 1872 and 1873 laws prohibiting discrimination in restaurants in Washington, D.C. With this knowledge, the CCEDA focused on increasing public awareness of the 1872 and 1873 laws and compelling city and federal officials to enforce the antidiscrimination laws already on the books. As part of that process, they gained airtime on the Tomlinson Todd radio show, a program broadcast in the district, in October 1949 on WOOK. The broadcast included guests Joseph Forer and Margaret A. Haywood, two attorneys who had studied the 1872 and 1873 civil rights laws; Ernest F. Harper, president of the D.C. Federation of Civic Associations; and Alice B. Hunter, secretary of the D.C. Recreation Board.[88]

The CCEDA was led by African American activist Mary Church Terrell (1863–1954), a daughter of former slaves. A native of Memphis, Tennessee, she moved to Washington, D.C., in 1890 and lived there until her death. In 1891, she married the notable D.C. lawyer Robert H. Terrell, who would go on to serve as the first African American municipal court judge in the nation's capital. In 1909, she and Ida B. Wells served as the only two women among the original founders of the NAACP. In 1913, she became one of the founding members of Delta Sigma Theta sorority. She also became a close friend of the noted abolitionist Frederick Douglass, who lived in the district at the end of his life, and together they worked on several civil rights campaigns.

Mary Church Terrell became one of the leaders of the movement to desegregate restaurants in the capital. "As a colored woman, I may walk from the Capitol to the White House," she said, "ravenously hungry and abundantly supplied with money with which to purchase a meal, without finding a single restaurant in which I would be permitted to take a morsel of food, if it was patronized by white people, unless I were willing to sit behind a screen."[89] She said that when a restaurant manager in the District of Columbia found an African American seated at one of the tables in his or her establishment and trying to order, the manager would cast them out like lepers.[90]

A LANDMARK COURT CASE

In January 1953, a racially mixed group of the CCEDA members tested the laws at a Thompson's Restaurant located at 723 Fourteenth Street in Northwest Washington, D.C. The Chicago-based John R. Thompson Company served as the ideal target for the group because it was the largest U.S. luncheonette chain of its time. In the 1920s, the Thompson's Restaurant chain operated 109 restaurants, 49 of them in Chicago and 11 in New York. It became one of the big three U.S. restaurant chains along with Childs and

The front of Thompson's Restaurant, 1935. *Courtesy of Pittsburgh City Photographer Collection, University of Pittsburgh.*

Waldorf Lunch. Thompson's had its own bakeries and among its popular menu items were Cervelat, smoked boiled tongue, cold boiled ham, hot dogs, corned beef, salmon and Herkimer County cheese served on "Milwaukee Rye Bread."[91]

MISS CHARLOTTE'S CHICKEN POT PIE

1 small stewing chicken
1 stalk celery
10 small white onions
2 tablespoons butter, softened
2 tablespoons flour
8 ½-inch unbaked baking powder biscuits

Disjoint and wash the fowl. Partly cover with water, add chopped celery and onions and simmer until just tender. Remove chicken, celery and onions from cooking liquid.

> Blend the softened butter with the flour and with this mixture thicken two cups of the liquid in which the chicken was cooked. When the sauce thickens, pour over the cooked chicken and vegetables in a deep baking dish. Cover with the unbaked biscuits and bake in a hot (400-degree) oven until the biscuits are well browned.
>
> *Modified from the* China Press, *September 11, 1936*

The CCEDA selected Thompson's precisely because it had been the largest luncheonette chain of its time with restaurants in several cities. The group that entered the Thompson's restaurant in the capital included Terrell, the Reverend Arthur F. Helms of People's Congregational Church and other unidentified members. The restaurant on Fourteenth Street refused service to Terrell and the other CCEDA members, and the group subsequently filed a suit in the District of Columbia Municipal Court. The court ruled in favor of the CCEDA. When the Thompson Company appealed the lower court's decision before the Municipal Court of Appeals, it was upheld by a 3–1 decision, saying that although the 1873 Act had repealed the 1872 Act, at least insofar as it applied to Thompson's Restaurant, the 1873 Act was still in effect. The Thompson's Restaurant chain petitioned the U.S. Court of Appeals to review the case. In a 5–4 decision, the court reversed the lower court's decision, thus repealing the "Equal Service Acts" passed by the legislative assembly of the District of Columbia and upheld by the District of Columbia Municipal Court in 1872 and again in 1873. "The 1872 and 1873 Acts made it a misdemeanor for the proprietor at any restaurant… ice cream parlor…or soda fountain to refuse service to any respectable, well-behaved person, without regard to race, color, or previous condition of servitude," reported the *Chicago Defender* on January 31, 1953, under the headline "High Court Scraps D.C. 'Lost Laws.'" Thus, in this landmark decision, the court deemed the nineteenth-century laws still valid, effectively ending legal support for discrimination in public places.

During court deliberations, several interesting facts about the 1872 and 1873 laws came out. First, under the old law, violators had to pay a fine of $100 and their license to do business was suspended for one year. Second, the U.S. Congress passed the Organic Act of 1878, which repealed the earlier Equal Service Acts.

The U.S. Court of Appeals approved racial "discrimination in restaurants and other places of public accommodation in the nation's capital" based on a code passed in 1901.[92] In response to the decision, the local chapter of the National Lawyers Guild; the American Veterans Committee; a group of prominent Washingtonians headed by Reverend A. Powell Davies, pastor of the All Souls Unitarian Church; and Rabbi Norman Gerstenfeld of the Washington Hebrew Congregation filed briefs as a friend of the court.[93]

ADAM CLAYTON POWELL JR.

Representative Adam Clayton Powell Jr. had gained a political base as an activist fighting against discrimination in restaurants in Harlem in the late 1930s. When he arrived in Washington in 1945, he found separate eateries on Capitol Hill and throughout the nation's capital. Powell became the first African American from New York to serve in the U.S. Congress and represented the Twenty-Second Congressional District, which included Harlem. When he arrived in Washington, Powell began inviting as many African Americans as he could "into the hitherto exclusive restaurant of the House of Representatives," he said.[94] In March 1945, Powell battled to desegregate the cafeteria on Capitol Hill. He introduced a resolution demanding that African American "employees of the federal government, serving in the capital, be admitted to the Capitol cafeteria." The resolution never gained traction, but "it achieved its purpose. Because the order went down: 'Stop Jim Crow in the United States Congressional facilities.'"[95]

Powell credits President Dwight D. Eisenhower with using the power of the executive office to desegregate restaurants throughout the capital. A record of Eisenhower's views on the Thompson case and whether they angered or inspired him to move against segregation does not exist; however, starting in March 1953, Eisenhower directed his ardent civil rights advocate and Attorney General Herbert Brownell Jr. to end "all segregation" in local restaurants. Sources on the strategy that Brownell used to carry out Eisenhower's wishes, including working through the Washington Restaurant Association (WRA), could not be found. Powell does tell us that after March 1953, the WRA would go on to report that "not one single case of serious friction arose."[96] Powell added, "The Board of Commissioners of the District of Columbia appointed by the President could have moved on many previous occasions to eliminate segregation....But the Commissioners did not move until they were urged by Eisenhower's Attorney General who pressured the newly appointed chairman to seek voluntary cooperation from the bars and restaurants in hotels of the city."[97] This action resulted in abolishing Jim Crow laws in the capital with the exception of discriminatory newspaper ads and some segregated housing.[98]

The available records show that the majority of restaurant owners did comply with serving black customers, although a lack of sources on the comfort level of African Americans now eating in newly integrated restaurants makes it harder to gauge how the transition went. As attorney general from January 1953 to November 1957, Brownell vigorously supported integration during the 1954 *Brown v. Board of Education* Supreme Court case, drafted the legislation that ultimately became the 1957 Civil Rights Act and recommended that President Eisenhower send federal troops to integrate Little Rock High School in Arkansas in September 1957.[99]

In his autobiography, Powell makes no claim that he influenced Eisenhower to act. He gives the impression that Eisenhower and his wife were progressive in terms of opposing Jim Crow policies in public facilities. However, President Eisenhower understood voting blocs and the necessity of not alienating white southern voters if possible. There is no evidence that Powell joined the CCEDA. As mentioned in the previous chapter, we do know that he held a leadership position in a similar organization in Harlem in the 1930s.

"I was born more than a half century ago, when [a] black stove was a place of magic where the coal fire always glowed and from which good things came," wrote Adam Clayton Powell. He went on to say,

> *I don't know how we modern men live on such paltry offerings—food then was food. For breakfast we had a different hot bread every morning—muffins, biscuits, corn bread, loaves of hot oatmeal bread with handfuls of raisins and blueberries sprinkled through them; pancakes so big that they seemed to be a yard wide but, in fact, were only the size of a big frying pan…and popovers so big you could put up your hand inside, which there was room for plenty of butter."*[100]

A popover is a hollow quick bread shaped like a muffin and made from a thin batter of eggs, milk and flour. Popovers evolved out of English pudding batters. Its popularity made its way from Maine to New York, and some recipes called for greasing the muffin tins with beef or pork drippings, creating a meat-flavored pastry. Other interpretations used garlic and herbs in the batter, and still others included substituting pureed pumpkin for some of the flour and flavoring the batter with allspice, nutmeg and cinnamon.[101] Today, most popovers have a butter flavor instead of meat or eggnog-like flavor.

Frugal cooks like Powell's mother, both then and now, try to reduce the amount of food they are throwing away and thereby reduce their food bill. To that end, they create ways to use leftovers. Powell said that his mother set the family menu based on "the law of diminishing returns. That is, whatever was bought for Sunday was bought with the objective that it should last in some form until Friday or Saturday, and it did." For his mother, "A fifteen-pound leg of mutton on a Sunday ended up on Friday or Saturday as lamb croquettes; during the intervening days it appeared as a ragout, stew, hash, and various and sundry other inventions."[102]

ROAST QUARTER OF LAMB

Procure a nice hind-quarter, remove some of the fat that is around the kidney, skewer the lower joint up to the fillet, place it in a moderate oven, let it heat through slowly, then dredge it with salt and flour; quicken the fire, put half a pint of water into the dripping-pan, with a teaspoonful of salt. With this liquor baste the meat occasionally; serve with lettuce, green peas and mint sauce. A quarter of lamb weighing seven or eight pounds will require two hours to roast.

A breast of lamb roasted is very sweet and is considered by many as preferable to hind-quarter. It requires nearly as long a time to roast as the quarter, and should be served in the same manner.

Make the gravy from the drippings, thickened with flour. The mint sauce is made as follows: Take fresh, young spearmint leaves stripped from stems; wash and drain them or dry on a cloth, chop very fine, put in a gravy tureen, and to three tablespoonful[s] of mint add two of finely powdered cut-loaf sugar; mix, and let it stand a few minutes, then pour over it six tablespoonful good cider or white-wine vinegar. The sauce should be made some time before dinner, so that the flavor of the mint may be well extracted.
—*Mrs. F.L. Gillette,* The Whitehouse Cookbook, *1887*

BROILING DIRECTIONS

Take off the shoulder and lay it upon the gridiron with the breast; cut in two parts, to facilitate its cooking; put a tin sheet on top of the meat, and a weight upon that; turn the meat around frequently to prevent its burning; turn over as soon as cooked on one side; renew the coals occasionally, that all parts may cook alike; when done, season with butter, pepper and salt—exactly like beefsteak. It takes some time to broil it well; but when done it will be found to be equal to broiled chicken, the flavor being more delicate than when cooked otherwise. Serve with cream sauce, made as follows: Heat a tablespoonful of butter in a saucepan, add a teaspoonful of flour and stir until perfectly smooth; then add, slowly stirring in, a cup of cold milk; let it boil up once, and season to taste with salt and pepper and a teaspoonful of finely chopped fresh parsley. Serve in a gravy boat, all hot.
—*Mrs. F.L. Gillette,* The Whitehouse Cookbook, *1887*

SCRAMBLED MUTTON

Two cups of chopped cold mutton, two tablespoonful[s] of hot water, and a piece of butter as large as an English walnut. When the meat is hot, break in three eggs, and

constantly stir until the eggs begin to stiffen. Season with pepper and salt.
　　—*Mrs. F.L. Gillette,* The Whitehouse Cookbook,
1887

SCALLOPED MUTTON AND TOMATOES

Over the bottom of an earthen baking-dish place a layer of bread crumbs, and over it alternate layers of cold roast mutton cut in thin slices, and tomatoes peeled and sliced; season each with salt, pepper and bits of butter, as laid in. The top layer should be of tomatoes, spread over with bread crumbs. Bake three-quarters of an hour, and serve immediately.
　　—*Mrs. F.L. Gillette,* The Whitehouse Cookbook,
1887

LAMB SWEETBREADS AND TOMATO SAUCE

Lamb sweetbreads are not always procurable, but a stroll through the markets occasionally reveals a small lot of them, which can invariably be had at a low price, owing to their excellence being recognized by but few buyers. Wash them well in salted water and parboil fifteen minutes; when cool, trim neatly and put them in a pan with just butter enough to prevent their burning; toss them about until a delicate color; season with salt and pepper and serve, surrounded with tomato sauce.
　　—*Mrs. F.L. Gillette,* The Whitehouse Cookbook, 1887

LAMB STEW

Cut up the lamb into small pieces (after removing all the fat) say about two inches square. Wash it well and put it over the fire, with just enough cold water to cover it well,

and let it heat gradually. It should stew gently until it is partly done; then add a few thin slices of salt pork, one or two onions sliced up fine, some pepper and salt if needed, and two or three raw potatoes cut up into inch pieces. Cover it closely and stew until the meat is tender. Drop in a few made dumplings, made like short biscuit, cut out very *small. Cook fifteen minutes longer. Thicken the gravy with a little flour moistened with milk. Serve.*
—*Mrs. F.L. Gillette,* The Whitehouse Cookbook, *1887*

PRESSED LAMB

The meat, either shoulder or leg, should be put to boil in the morning with water just enough to cover it; when tender, season with salt and pepper, then keep it over the fire until very *tender and the juice nearly boiled out. Remove it from the fire-place in a wooden chopping bowl, season more if necessary, chop it up like hash. Place it in a bread-pan, press out all the juice, and put it in a cool place to harden. The pressing is generally done by placing a dish over the meat and putting a flat-iron upon that. Nice cut up cold into thin slices, and the broth left from the meat would make a nice soup served with it, adding vegetables and spices.*
—*Mrs. F.L. Gillette,* The Whitehouse Cookbook, *1887*

LAMB CROQUETTES

These are made of any scraps or bits of good food that happen to be left from one or more meals, and in such small quantities that they cannot be warmed up separately. As, for example, a couple of spoonful of frizzled beef and cream, the lean meat of one mutton chop, one spoonful of minced beef, two cold hard-boiled eggs, a little cold chopped potato, a little mashed potato, a chick's leg, all the gristle and hard outside taken from the meat. These things well chopped and seasoned, mixed with one raw egg, a little flour and butter, and boiling water; then made into round cakes, thick like fish-balls and browned well with butter in a frying pan or on a griddle.

Scraps of hash, cold rice, and boiled oatmeal left from breakfast, every kind of fresh meat, bits of salt tongue, bacon, pork or ham, bits of poultry, and crumbs of bread may be used. They should be put together with care, so as not to have them too dry to be palatable, or too moist to cook in shape. Most housekeepers would be surprised at the result, making an addition to the breakfast or lunch table. Serve on small squares of buttered toast, and with cold celery if in season.

—*Mrs. F.L. Gillette,* The Whitehouse Cookbook, *1887*

THE "CLUB FROM NOWHERE"

To name the typical food product of Alabama is more difficult than to name some of Alabama's characteristic dishes. And even more typical of this State is the arrangement of foods in a single menu which, wherever served, speaks eloquently of Southern cooking as it is known in the cotton and corn State. Those who swear by our cooking, and there are some in every community, will agree with the sentiment expressed in the verse that cooking is like religion—"some's selected an'some ain't." Nevertheless, I hope to be able to give directions to those who are ambitious to win the enviable reputation that Southern cooks have always had. —food writer Louise Glanton, "Alabama Menus and Recipes: Genuine, Tasty Southern Cooking as Found in the State of Cotton and Corn," Baltimore Sun, *October 19, 1930.*

MLK, THE MONTGOMERY BUS BOYCOTT AND THE MONTGOMERY IMPROVEMENT ASSOCIATION

When Montgomery authorities arrested black bus passenger Rosa Parks on December 1, 1955, for refusing to give up her seat to a white passenger, just about the entire black community of the city rallied to her aid. E.D. Nixon, president of the Montgomery NAACP and an active member of A. Philip Randolph's Pullman Porters Union, organized a meeting of the city's black leaders.[103]

To ensure solidarity among this often fragmented group, they agreed on Martin Luther King Jr. (MLK), a newcomer with impeccable credentials, to serve as the president and the voice of the newly established Montgomery Improvement Association (MIA). MLK had graduated from Morehouse College with a bachelor's degree in sociology and left the South in 1948 to attend graduate school. He graduated from Crozer Theological Seminary in Pennsylvania with a masters of divinity degree in 1951 and earned his doctorate of philosophy in systematic theology from Boston University in 1955. It was while he was studying in Boston that he met his future wife, Coretta Scott, who was attending the New England Conservatory of Music.[104]

MLK's father led the Ebenezer Baptist Church in Atlanta, Georgia, and became a leader of the civil rights movement as the head of the city's NAACP chapter and of the Civic and Political League. King Sr. encouraged his son to become active in the movement. MLK's baptism into nonviolence and passive resistance occurred at his first and only full-time pastorate at the Dexter Avenue Baptist Church in Montgomery, Alabama, where he served from 1954 to 1960. (He completed his PhD requirements during his first year in Montgomery.) In addition to performing his administrative and pastoral duties, he strongly encouraged his congregation to take an active role in the resolution of current civic/social problems. Two of his members, Jo Ann Robinson and Rufus Lewis, were among the first people to become critical players in the Montgomery Bus Boycott. King Sr. insisted that every church member become a registered voter, a member of the NAACP and a participating member of the church's Social and Political Action Committee, designed to keep the congregation engaged in bringing about progressive change. The church was the place where MLK first preached his message of hope and brotherhood, and it became the center point of the Montgomery bus boycott. The MIA declared a boycott of the bus system beginning on December 5, and MLK became a prominent civil rights leader as international attention focused on Montgomery.[105]

GEORGIA GILMORE AND THE "CLUB FROM NOWHERE" SUPPORT THE MOVEMENT

A cook with the National Lunch Company, Georgia Gilmore (1920–1990) was described as kind and motherly but was also known for her temper, especially in response to the racial injustices so common at the time. "I was the kind of person who would be fiery," she said. "I didn't mind fighting you. I didn't care if you were white or black." When Gilmore heard of the arrest on the news, she quickly joined the MIA. Her involvement in the boycott, along with her vocal contempt for discriminatory white bus drivers, resulted in her being fired from the National Lunch Company.[106]

In Montgomery, King lived just three blocks from Gilmore, who was already a renowned cook in the area. He knew from personal experience that the cook put her foot in it (that's southern for someone who really can cook!). Following Gilmore's dismissal from her job, MLK and other MIA leaders gave her the capital necessary to start a catering business and restaurant out of her home as a way for her to make a living.[107]

It was then that Gilmore began the boycott fundraising effort that would help feed the revolution. Women, who were not invited to the MIA organizing meeting, organized their own groups, with Gilmore taking the lead. The maids and cooks of Montgomery served as the most important patrons of the public bus system. When these women joined the boycott, the buses remained almost empty. The majority of them had jobs in the segregated Cloverdale, Capitol Heights and Oak Park sections of the city. During the boycott, they walked and rode in MIA carpools instead of riding the bus.[108]

In order to keep the carpool running and make the boycott a success, Gilmore and other African American women who supported the boycott organized a baking club on the east and west sides of the city and named it "the club from nowhere" (TCN).[109] The club name allowed them to earn money for the movement without raising the suspicion of white officials and members of the Klan. A lot of white citizens in Montgomery purchased baked goods from club members not knowing that they had inadvertently supported the MIA's boycott. In addition to selling baked goods, the clubs collected donations from people who didn't attend the mass meetings but wanted to give donations to help keep the carpool going.[110]

Women fed members of the MIA who spent extra time walking to work and thus had little time for cooking. For slightly above cost, MIA members could eat in or take a plate home of "meatloaf with cream potatoes, cheese and macaroni, rutabagas, peas with okra, lettuce and tomato, apple pie, and iced tea," recalled Gilmore.[111] She had both black and white customers and folks from all walks of life who came to love her fried chicken, macaroni and cheese, stuffed pork chops, stuffed peppers and chitlins with coleslaw. She and the TCN literally fed the MIA's 1955 revolution.[112]

GEORGE WASHINGTON CARVER'S SWEET POTATO BREAD

By the 1930s, George Washington Carver had become recognized as one of the leading food scientists in the United States. This was quite unusual considering he carried on his work in the South during a period when popular white public opinion viewed African Americans as weak-minded. Carver spent most of his career on the faculty of Tuskegee Institute in Tuskegee Alabama–a historically black college that the former slave and noted educator Booker T. Washington founded just after the Civil War. Carver would go on to receive the Theodore Roosevelt medal for his achievements in food science, including discovering over two hundred different uses for the sweet potato. Carver often said that anybody could cook with sweet potatoes, which he described as "pleasant with a delicate flavor if cooked properly." About the sweet potato, Carver also said, "Steaming develops and preserves the flavor better than boiling and baking better than steaming. A sweet potato cooked quickly is not cooked. Time is an essential element."[113]

1 teaspoon salt
1 cup finely mashed sweet potatoes
½ teaspoon yeast cake
2 tablespoons warm water
3¾ cups flour, or sufficient to make soft dough

Add the salt to the potatoes and the yeast; put in the water and flour, enough to make a smooth sponge (about a cupful). Cover and set in a warm place to rise. When light, add the remainder of the flour or whatever is needed to make a smooth, elastic dough. Cover and let rise until light. Shape into loaves or rolls; let rise and bake. Many variations of the above bread can be made by adding sugar, butter, lard, nuts and spices.

Modified from the Afro-American, *December 9, 1939*

New Journal & Guide food editor Arden H. Duane had this to say about what she considered a superb pie recipe: "Ah, how I enjoyed that pie! Such apple pie I have never tasted. Apple pie, a perennial favorite with men, will just endear you all to their hearts forever and a day. Try this recipe then write and tell me honestly where and when you have tasted better apple pie."

APPLE PIE

2 pie paste crusts
4 to 6 tart and juicy apples, thinly sliced
¾ cup sugar
1 teaspoon lemon juice
1 teaspoon cinnamon or nutmeg (as desired)
1 tablespoon fine brandy
1 tablespoon butter

Line a pan with pie paste crust (a puff pastry) and fill with thinly sliced apples. Add the sugar, lemon juice, spice and brandy. Dot with butter. Cover with the top crust, cutting a few slips to allow steam to escape. Bake 10 minutes in a hot (400-degree) oven. Reduce heat slightly and bake for 30 minutes more.

Modified from New Journal & Guide, *November 9, 1935*

BAKED MACARONI AND CHEESE

"Baked macaroni and cheese is the big, American, easy to prepare supper dish for meatless day and other occasions," wrote Venus Shepherd, a food writer for the *Afro-American* and a native of Montgomery Alabama. In April, hundreds of Christian housewives in the South would comb the food sections of their newspapers in search of meatless dishes in observance of the Lenten season. Some families abstained from meat during the entire Lenten season while others abstained on Wednesdays and Fridays during Lent. Those charged with making meals for the family had to be creative in order to keep family members from grumbling about the lack of meat. Popular meatless dishes included fish (which church officials deemed acceptable), soups, stews, legumes and pasta prepared in myriad ways, including macaroni and cheese.

Makes 6 servings

8 ounces elbow macaroni
¼ cup fat
1 teaspoon minced onion
¼ cup flour
1 teaspoon salt
⅛ teaspoon pepper
⅛ teaspoon dry mustard
1½ cups milk
1 cup (4 ounces) grated American cheese
1 3-ounce can sliced cooked mushrooms
2 tablespoons sherry wine, optional

Cook macaroni until barely tender in boiling salted water. Meanwhile, place saucepan over medium heat with fat. Add onion and cook for 1 minute. Stir in flour, salt, pepper and mustard. Add milk and cook, stirring constantly until the sauce thickens. Add cheese and continue to stir until cheese melts. Remove from the heat and stir in mushrooms. Add sherry, if desired. Drain macaroni and place in a greased, shallow baking dish. Pour sauce over macaroni, mixing gently with fork if necessary. Bake at 375 degrees Fahrenheit, until brown as desired. Serve hot.

Modified from the Afro-American, *April 9, 1949*

In order to keep riders off the bus, the MIA had to come up with its own transportation system to get its members to work—many of them maids and cooks for Montgomery's white establishment. Georgia Gilmore and the various members of TCN sold fresh baked goods around the city with the proceeds helping keep the MIA transportation network rolling. The women

A woman sells baked goods. *Courtesy of Library of Congress.*

Several women sell cakes. *Courtesy of Library of Congress.*

of the TCN baked the pies and cakes that provided the essential funds for the carpool to shuttle its members to work and purchase cars, gas and picket signs in support of the boycott.[114]

BLUEBERRY PIE

3 tablespoons quick-cooking tapioca
¾ to 1 cup sugar
¼ teaspoon salt
4 cups fresh blueberries
1 tablespoon lemon juice
pastry dough for two pie crusts
1 tablespoon butter

Combine quick-cooking tapioca, sugar, salt, berries and lemon juice and let stand for 15 minutes while you prepare the pastry dough. Line a 9-inch pie pan with half the pastry rolled an ⅛ inch thick and cut into ½-inch strips. Fill pie shell with berry mixture and dot with butter. Moisten edge of bottom crust with cold water. Adjust pastry strips and lattice across top of pie and flatten rim with fingers. Bake in hot oven set at 450 degrees Fahrenheit for 45 minutes, or until syrup boils with heavy bubbles that do not burst. Note: if desired, a cup of granulated sugar and ½ cup brown sugar may be substituted for the ¾ to 1 cup granulated sugar.

Modified from the Afro-American, *July 19, 1952*

SAUTTER'S OLD-FASHIONED POUND CAKE

By 1939, the Sautter family of Philadelphia, Pennsylvania, had been in the restaurant and catering business for more than fifty years. When the last member of the Sautter clan decided to close the family business, locals prevailed on businessman Jasper G. Lopez to continue the business and the production of its prized pound cake. When Lopez bought the business, the pound cake recipe and Jacob Yackle, a baker who had worked for the Sautters since 1918 and knew all the family recipes by heart, came as part of a packaged deal.

1 pound butter
1 pound sugar

THE "CLUB FROM NOWHERE"

1 pound eggs, separated
1 tablespoon vanilla extract
2 teaspoons orange extract
1 pound all-purpose flour, sifted

Cream butter and beat in sugar gradually. Cream together well. Add the egg yolks bit by bit and continue beating until thoroughly blended. Add flavorings and lightly fold in flour. Beat egg whites until just barely stiff, fold again and oh so gently. Pour into two loaf pans lined with heavy waxed paper and buttered. Bake 1½ hours in moderate oven (325 degrees Fahrenheit).

Modified from Baltimore Sun, *February 5, 1950*

Their customers included both whites and blacks who purchased heavenly tasting food at cab stands, barbershops and beauty salons. In a friendly, competitive spirit, the presidents of TCN clubs on each side of the city would announce at the regular mass meetings held at Holt Street Baptist Church how much their respective clubs earned and gave to the MIA, leading to loud applauses, praise and jubilation. "The Club from Nowhere was able to collect maybe $150 to $200 or more a week," Gilmore said. "I collected the money and I'd always report it at the mass meetings, the same day that they would give it to us, so there was never any conflict."[115]

Gilmore's makeshift restaurant also served as a critical space where MIA leaders like King, E.D. Nixon, Ralph Abernathy and others held strategy meetings. It was free

Martin Luther King Jr., speaking at a rally.
Courtesy of Library of Congress.

of wiretaps, which white authorities were using to gather intelligence on the MIA. White folks knew better than to mess with Gilmore. A large woman, almost 350 or more pounds, who moved quickly on her feet, she once got in a fight with a local male white merchant who refused to refund her money after selling one of her children a stale loaf of bread.[116]

MLK viewed Gilmore and her restaurant as essential to the movement. He would bring VIPs like Bobby Kennedy there for a great meal in a safe space. He would also often retreat there to a get a good and safe home-cooked meal.[117]

The *China Press* of September 11, 1936, published an anonymous article titled "Fowls in Southern Style" that discussed the southern love affair with chicken dishes:

> *There's much plain and fancy raving done about good old Southern chicken dishes. People who can't locate Baltimore in relation to [the] Chesapeake Bay grow dreamy-eyed and poetic as they describe Maryland fried chicken. Northerners to whom "mammy" means no more than a song and a pair of white gloves, go into ecstasies over the joys of an authentic Dixie chicken shortcake. A great deal of the lore of fine Southern cookery has long since drifted over the Mason-Dixon line. But it still seems likely that there's news yet to be spread when it comes to the creation of the superb chicken dishes. At least, so our mail bag would indicate.*

SMOTHERED CHICKEN

1 young chicken
⅛ pound butter
1 teaspoon lemon juice or vinegar
1 teaspoon salt
2 cups hot water, plus more as needed
½ cup flour, plus 3 tablespoons
3 tablespoons butter
salt, to taste
white pepper (optional), to taste

Open young chicken down the back, and clean as usual. Lay the chicken flat in a baking dish with the skin down. Into the hollows put butter, lemon juice or vinegar and salt. Into the pan put hot water. Be careful to keep the water up to that amount during the cooking. Set in a moderate (350-degree) oven and baste from time to time with liquid in the pan. After 30 minutes, turn the chicken over, dredge with flour and cover. Baste frequently. Cook until tender. Mix together equal parts butter and flour. To this, add ½ cup liquid from the pan. When well mixed, return all to the pan and stir till the gravy is thickened. Be careful to get plenty of salt to taste. A little white pepper may be desired.

Modified from the Baltimore Sunday, *October 19, 1930*

ALABAMA CHICKEN STEW

2 small chickens
salt and pepper, to taste
3 tablespoons butter
2 tablespoons flour, divided
2 cups water, plus 1 tablespoon
2 small onions, sliced
1 sprig parsley
1 stalk celery, chopped
½ bay leaf
½ teaspoon curry powder
2 cups cooking sherry
2 egg yolks

Disjoint the chickens and rub with salt and pepper. Melt butter on the stove. Brown the chicken slowly in the melted butter. Sift in 1 tablespoon flour, and then add the water, onions, parsley, celery, bay leaf and curry powder mixed with sherry. Cover and simmer for 45 minutes. Beat the egg yolks with the remaining tablespoon of flour and the tablespoon of cold water. Remove the pieces of chicken and arrange on a hot platter. Pour a small amount of the hot liquid into the egg mixture, whisking constantly. Then add eggs to the liquid on the stovetop to thicken for a minute. Strain the sauce and pour over the chicken to serve.

Modified from the China Press, *September 11, 1936*

The Montgomery bus boycott lasted thirteen months and ended with the U.S. Supreme Court ruling that segregation on public buses is unconstitutional. The bus boycott demonstrated the potential for nonviolent mass protest to successfully challenge racial segregation and served as an example for other southern campaigns that followed.

Martin Luther King played a key role in maintaining solidarity among the often fragmented leadership of the MIA. In addition, his oratory helped maintain the morale of the rank-and-file members of the MIA. No doubt, these were important roles during the Montgomery bus boycott, but ultimately, the success of the boycott depended on the discipline, endurance and sacrifice of large numbers of domestic servants and cooks. Without these people agreeing to walk instead of ride on the buses, the boycott would have failed. When a reporter asked one such domestic how she was holding up with so much walking during the thirteen-month boycott, she responded, "My feet is tired, but my soul is rested."

4

A NOTE OF SUPPORT
WITH YOUR FOOD

A portion of this chapter is given in great detail in my previous work Upsetting the Apple Cart: Black and Latino Coalitions in New York From Protest to Public Office *(Columbia University Press, 2015).*

During the 1950s and '60s, hospital service jobs were filled by the working poor. These workers—janitors, cooks, maintenance staff and nurse's aides—earned some of the lowest wages in the country. It's no surprise that the vast majority of them were black or Latino. One of the draws of these jobs was that hospitals often overlooked employees' immigration status. In New York City between 1960 and 1970, blacks and Latinos constituted 80 percent of the hospital service and maintenance workforce.[118] They shared one goal: needing to pay the bills. In the hospitals, workers of different races and ethnicities held similar positions and had the same struggles. Worker solidarity increased as workers talked and ate together in hospital cafeterias and then started meeting in union halls, at rallies, on picket lines and in one another's homes.

Service workers' union Local 1199 began organizing workers at New York's nonprofit hospitals starting in 1959. Workers went on strike several times over the next few years. White labor leaders; Hispanic activists, unionists and political leaders; black unionists and nationalists; and civil rights leaders all played a role in the fight. By 1962, workers had gained union recognition and collective bargaining rights.

HOSPITAL FOOD

The first big turn of events in the organizing drive for hospital workers came when one hospital administration decided to end its long-standing meal plan. Workers at Montefiore Medical Center in the Bronx had allowed workers to eat in the cafeteria and then deducted the cost of these "free meals" from workers' paychecks.[119] When the hospital hired Jacques Bloch to lead its new food service department in 1954, he reorganized the department, opened a new cafeteria and ended the free food policy within three years. In their book, *Upheaval in the Quiet Zone: A History of Hospital Workers' Union, Local 1199*, historians Leon Fink and Brian Greenberg argue that the decision "increased the amount of take-home pay for workers but still triggered resentments."[120] That may be true, but the real issue seems to have been that the quality and quantity of food provided by the hospital was greater than what workers could procure independently with their slightly increased take-home pay. In addition, the hospital cafeteria served as a de facto restaurant for many workers who could not afford to eat out, giving it great cultural and social significance.

Ken Downs, who worked on the lunch line, was the first to recognize that this change could be the thing to galvanize workers. A Barbadian, Downs had some experience with labor unions and politics in his home region of St. Joseph's parish in Barbados and later in Trinidad. He migrated and for ten years worked in Trinidad, where he did carpentry and painting and worked as a cook before operating his own food stand selling prepared foods. At the age of forty-five, he migrated to New York City "to better his conditions," said Downs.[121] He moved in with an elder brother, a World War I veteran who had settled in Harlem. The brother worked as an elevator operator on Fourteenth Street and owned "a lot of houses in Harlem."[122] Hospital officials at Montefiore hired Downs to work in their food department as a cook in 1950, the same year he migrated from Trinidad.

After the free food program was eliminated, Downs contacted 1199 staffers to start an organizing movement. He told Elliot Godoff that they couldn't lose because the workers are "paying for the food."[123] Downs got on his supervisor's bad side for not letting the supervisor push the Puerto Ricans around. Because of that, Downs insisted that Puerto Ricans in the kitchen would "fight anybody" who tried to mess with him. As he said, "I get along with them well."[124] Quite early on, Downs started attending 1199 informational meetings and quickly gained a reputation as a great cook and "union man."[125] He even won a union prize for the most new registrants and became a shop steward. He regularly "used to go to every floor at night and sign" up workers to join the union and soon, he said, "everybody would come to me for information."[126]

At Montefiore, Downs prepared breakfast on the grill and served lunch on the food line. "[I cooked] seventy-two eggs at once and eighteen or twenty… big pancakes," said Downs. Working on the grill and lunch line, Downs had the opportunity to get to know a lot of workers, as "they had to come through the line to me," he said.[127] He added, "But we met in homes when we…first started to organize." Downs explained, "We had a party, and I cooked chicken and rice and peas." The home meetings as an organizing strategy lasted for four weeks, with Downs catering the event.[128] Many of the lab technicians whom Downs met as they came through the line attended the organizing home meetings. The lowest paid workers joined the union first, but they would not have organized, argued Downs, if hospital officials had not stopped the free food. "All these hospitals used to do it," he said. "And if that didn't stop, I doubt a union would be in there today."[129]

CARIBBEAN MIGRANTS AND CARIBBEAN FOOD

The migration of large numbers of blacks from the southern United States and the Caribbean to New York during World War I and II contributed to the introduction of various foods and dishes. Immigrants from these two regions have made an indelible mark on the local cuisine, adding dishes like fried chicken and fried plantains, meat patties, jerked and curried meats and rice and beans. Historically, every region of the American South and the Caribbean has had a different take on rice-and-bean dishes. One such example is Downs's Barbadian rice and peas.

Regional Rifts on Fried Chicken

A 1960s article in the *Baltimore Sun* tells us that there is but one basic fried chicken recipe that cooks across the Americas use as their basis, in a manner similar to a talented jazz artist improvising on a common chord progression. In Kentucky, for example, cooks serve fried chicken with hot pancakes smothered with brown gravy. It is fried chicken and waffles in Virginia smothered in white gravy. In Georgia, they do fried chicken with grits, rice or whipped sweet potatoes. Gulf Coast cooks in the South rub lemon on the skin of the chicken before pan frying it and serving it most often with red beans and rice. This is the style, for example, in New Orleans.

BASIC FRIED CHICKEN

1 plump, young chicken
salt
pepper
flour
fat or oil

Cut chicken in serving pieces. Season with salt and pepper and roll in the flour. Heat fat (about 1½ inches deep) in a heavy frying pan. Put the thickest pieces of chicken in fat first. Do not crowd—leave enough space for the fat to come up around each piece. Cook slowly, turning often. Do not cover pan. The thickest pieces will take from 20 to 35 minutes to cook. After the pieces have been browned, cooking may be finished in a moderate oven (350 degrees Fahrenheit) if more convenient.

Modified from the Baltimore Sun, January 29, 1960

RICE AND BEANS AND PEAS AND RICE

Everywhere Africans disembarked in the Americas, they developed rice and beans, as well as peas and rice, dishes similar to what they ate in West Africa. Rice and legumes provided Africans with an inexpensive and nutritious food combination that they could easily grow in their subsistence gardens.[130] The Works Progress Administration (WPA) project "America Eats," which was never published, reveals that Latin Americans, West Indians and African Americans often frequented the same restaurants in Harlem and the Upper West Side. You could go to a Cuban or Puerto Rican restaurant and eat rice and beans along with bread and butter for thirty-five cents. After Cubop began to catch on in New York City in 1947, it became common to see Latino and African Americans frequenting the same jazz venues and afterward enjoying traditional southern and Caribbean food.

The blending and sharing of black and Hispanic music and food extended beyond Harlem to the other four boroughs of New York City, particularly to the Bronx, Brooklyn and Queens.

HAITIAN RED BEANS AND RICE

Serves 6

1 cup dry red beans
8 cups water
1 teaspoon salt, plus additional to taste
1 onion, diced
1 small green pepper, sliced
salt pork, sausage, bacon or ham bone (optional)
1½ cups bean-cooking water
2 tablespoons shortening
1 cup long-grain rice
1 teaspoon lemon juice
pepper, to taste

Pick over beans carefully, discarding imperfect specimens. Wash, cover with fresh cold water and soak overnight.

Drain and then gently cook uncovered in boiling salted water with onion and pepper for two hours, or until tender. If desired, small pieces of salt pork, sausage, bacon or a ham bone may be cooked with the beans. After cooking, drain and reserve 1 ½ cups of the bean-cooking water.

Heat one tablespoon shortening in a frying pan. Add beans, pepper and onion; fry until slightly browned.

Wash rice thoroughly. Bring the reserved cooking water to a boil. Add rice slowly so boiling doesn't cease. Add lemon juice, salt and pepper. Simmer gently without stirring until water steams vigorously and is down to rice level. Add remaining tablespoon shortening. Reduce heat as low as possible. Cover kettle and cook until rice is thoroughly tender, dry and fluffy. Mix with fried beans.

Modified from Baltimore Sun, *October 2, 1949*

The "Best Cake maker" in New York City is a man! He is
Allen Mulberry, of Manhattan, who is married and the
father of four children and expects another momentarily. Mr.
Mulberry baked the cakes that won both first and third prizes
in the Cake making contest of the *New York Amsterdam News*
Home-Food Show at the 369th Armory on October 1, 2, and
3. He is a native of Palatka, Fla., where his Godmother, Mrs.
Orlanda Brinson taught him to cook at 11 years of age in her
restaurant—the "Brunson Street Restaurant."
—*New York Amsterdam News*, October 17, 1959

PINEAPPLE DELIGHT

FOR THE CAKE
10 eggs
1 cup sugar
2½ cups flour
1 teaspoon baking powder
pinch salt

Whip eggs and sugar together. Fold in flour, baking powder
and salt. Bake in two layers at 350 degrees Fahrenheit for
25 to 30 minutes, until a toothpick inserted in the center
comes out clean. Allow to cool as you prepare the custard
and icing.

FOR THE CUSTARD
2½ cups milk
1 cup sugar
3 eggs
3 tablespoons cornstarch
2 tablespoons butter

Boil 2 cups milk and half the sugar in a double boiler. Mix
the remainder of the sugar, the eggs and cornstarch and
add to the boiling milk. Stir constantly until smooth. Then
add butter. Let cool and add the last ½ cup milk.

FOR THE ICING
3 cups powdered sugar
2 cups butter
pinch salt
1 tablespoon rum flavor

Mix sugar and butter with salt and flavoring. Beat until smooth.

TO ASSEMBLE
2 layers prepared cake
custard
1½ cups cooked pineapple
icing

Place first cake layer on a plate or cake dish, trimming the top of it isn't level. Spread the custard mixture evenly over the layer. Top custard with an even layer of cooked pineapple. Place the second layer of cake on the pineapple and custard and trim the top if it isn't level. Place ½ to ⅓ of the icing on the top of the cake and spread with an offset spatula to cover the cake, adding more icing as needed.

Modified from the New York Amsterdam News, *October 17, 1959*

PEPPER RELISH
Yields 3 pints

12 red peppers
12 green peppers
4 medium-sized onions
1 small cabbage
2 cups sugar
2 cups vinegar
2 tablespoons salt
1 tablespoon celery salt

Split peppers and remove seeds. Coarsely chop peppers, onions and cabbage. Cover with boiling water and let stand for 5 minutes. Drain. Cover again with boiling water and let stand for 10 minutes. Drain. Combine remaining ingredients in a saucepan and boil for 10 minutes. Add vegetables and cook for 40 minutes. Pack in hot, sterilized jars and seal.

Modified from the New York Amsterdam News, *July 12, 1958*

YAMS FLAMB

2 red yams
¼ cup butter
salt
¼ cup brown sugar
2 jiggers of Jamaica rum

First, scrub two large red yams and boil them in their skins until they are barely tender. Peel and cut them in ½-inch slices, and then cook them in the blazer or the chafing dish with butter until they're brown on both sides. Sprinkle the potatoes with salt and brown sugar. Pour on Jamaica rum. As soon as the rum is hot, light it. Serve when the flames die out.

Modified from the Philadelphia Tribune, *November 7, 1959*

JAMAICA FRITTERS

4 apples
Jamaica rum
flour
butter
powdered sugar

About 3 or 4 hours before dinner, peel and core apples and cut them in ½-inch slices. Cover them with Jamaica

---

rum and let them stand. Just before dinner is ready to be served, drain the apple slices (save that rum!) and dip them in flour, shaking off any surplus. Sauté the apple slices in plenty of butter in the blazer of the chafing dish (a portable, elevated grate on a tripod used to gently cook food using indirect heat) and serve them piping hot with powdered sugar and rum sauce. If you prefer, the slices can be dipped in thin fritter batter (recipe follows) instead of in the flour. In this case, they should be dried before dipping.

Modified from the Philadelphia Tribune, *November 7, 1959*

FRITTER BATTER

2 eggs, well beaten
⅔ cup milk
1 tablespoon rum
1 tablespoon butter
½ teaspoon salt
1 cup flour

Mix all ingredients well.

Modified from the Philadelphia Tribune, *November 7, 1959*

COMING TOGETHER AND FEEDING THE PROTESTERS

Born in Columbus, Ohio, Thelma Bowles moved to New York in 1931, when she was twenty-one. She lived and worked in New Jersey for several years before entering Montefiore's licensed practical nurse (LPN) training school in 1950. After graduating, she started working the night shift in the hospital's nursing department.

Bowles helped organize LPNs and nurse's aides, who at the time were largely African American and English-speaking people from the Caribbean. To organize workers on the day shift, she would sometimes come into the hospital around lunchtime and talk with them in the hospital cafeteria. Multiethnic subgroups of workers tended to eat together in the cafeteria based on their occupations: nurses with nurses, doctors with doctors and members of the hospital kitchen department with other members of the hospital kitchen department. Bowles and other organizers invited Montefiore workers to a union-sponsored lunch at the makeshift headquarters on Gun Hill Road during an undisclosed month in 1958. She and three other nightshift workers went to Bowles's house the morning of the lunch to prepare sandwiches for the event. "We'd make the sandwiches and then I would pack them in a box and I would take them to the union headquarters for the luncheon," Bowles recalled. "I remember that Mo [Foner, 1199's former public relations director] was on the phone calling me, 'Bring more sandwiches, bring more sandwiches!'" Bowles said, "We were working like beavers trying to get these sandwiches" to all the workers who had heard about the free lunch and packed the union hall.[131]

The Gun Hill Road headquarters became an important place for Montefiore workers to "drop in and talk to anyone if they wanted to," explained Bowles. It was within walking distance of the hospital, and workers could come by, "hear what the union organizers had to say" and ask questions.[132] That Bronx union hall also played a crucial role in building solidarity among workers of different ethnic and racial backgrounds. In the hospital, workers often remained separated according to clearly established occupational hierarchies. At the union hall, however, workers "began to know each other [as equals]....By the time of the strike, everybody was like real brothers and sisters."[133]

The union organized a strike vote in March 1959. Multiracial coalitions worked together around the clock in support of the strike. Shortly after the start of the strike, labor leader Harry Van Arsdale called a meeting of all the unions in the city to develop a strategy for supporting the striking workers. Officials went back to their local unions and asked their members to support everyone on the picket lines. "These strikers are human beings [underline in the original], no matter what their color or country of origin," labor leaders from Local 585 stated in a letter sent to members on May 13, 1959. "Many of them are on WELFARE DEPARTMENT [capitalizations in the original] relief, so they can afford to buy just the food, clothing, and shelter to keep them and their families alive when they are working. The hospitals refuse to understand...and threaten the union with fines, jail, and the strikers [living in hospital-owned housing] with eviction notices and the threat of no jobs to return to....YOU CAN HELP THEM WIN THIS STRIKE!" Local 585 and many other unions encouraged their members to bring "canned food or [send] cash, check, or money order to us to be given to Local 1199 FOOD FUND." They also asked members to send the striking workers "a note of support with your food or dollars to let them know that you believe in what they are doing." The letter ended with: "This fight for rights is expected to continue for a lengthy period as more hospitals join in the strike. Give at least once, but please remember the need for food is three (3) times a day for these people, so keep the food and money coming in, and you will have the blessings of these unfortunate people."[134] In total, 175 unions responded to Van Arsdale's call for support, and contributions poured into 1199 headquarters.

The financial support from other unions allowed 1199's staff to distribute

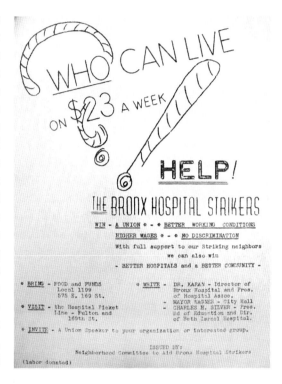

A strike support flyer. *Courtesy of Kheel Center, Cornell University.*

food, money for transportation and free medical care to striking workers. The brewery trade unions and the Building Services Employees Union joined picket lines and brought food. The bakery workers brought fresh-baked breads, cakes and rolls. The Amalgamated Meat Cutters and Butchers Workmen of North America donated two weeks' worth of meat to every hospital worker out on strike and provided cold cuts to strike headquarters for sandwiches. Members of the Transport Workers Union contributed thousands of cans of food and walked on picket lines. The International Brotherhood of Electrical Workers made the largest donation: $28,115, forty-eight thousand eggs and four thousand chickens.[135]

The striking workers had plenty of food, but they had a problem trying to feed people because the nearby union hall had no cooking facilities. A Democratic club or some kind of social club near Mount Sinai Hospital had a kitchen a block away that let striking workers use it. Workers shopped in the mornings for food and then later in the day cooked big meals in large pots and kettles. Those on the picket line would take turns coming in off the streets to eat a hot meal. The community around Mount Sinai also joined in solidarity with the striking hospital workers donating canned foods.[136]

The 1199 received so many food donations that it created a makeshift grocery store for the striking workers. It gave away large bags of food with chicken and rice and bread that Zoro Bread Company of New York donated every day. The majority of the food came from pro-union Jewish merchants, bakers and butchers. Latino and African American merchants also made donations. Ted Mitchell, 1199's first full-time African American labor organizer, remembered distributing "bags of food" filled with fresh bread, poultry, meat, eggs and canned foods to striking workers every week.[137] Mount Sinai employee Olivia Barney recalled, "They gave us beans, peas, and sugar. We and the Puerto Ricans were bean people, so that was good."[138]

SOUTHERN BEANS

pinto beans
dash pepper
salt
1 small onion, minced
bacon

Take pinto beans and add pepper, salt, onion and bacon. Bring to a boil and then reduce heat, cooking down until thickened.

Modified from the Baltimore Afro-American, *August 28, 1965*

In 1962, workers pursuing union representation in contract negotiations and grievances at Beth-El Hospital and Manhattan Eye, Ear and Throat Institute went on strike. The judge again delivered an injunction against 1199. In addition, the judge had 1199 president Leon Davis incarcerated for thirty days. He continued to support the strike after his jail time ended, so the judge sentenced him to six additional months behind bars. A. Philip Randolph, the vice-president of the American Federation of Labor and Congress of Industrial Organizations (AFL-CIO), put his substantial political capital and organizing skills toward assisting Davis and the striking workers.

Throughout his long career, Randolph, who was African American, put a premium on unity as a way to advance the labor movement's objectives. To that end, he contacted civil rights leaders, ministers and state officials asking for their support in battling what he called "the most dramatic form [of] second-class citizenship status and sweatshop wages of all minority group workers in our city."[139]

Bayard Rustin, Randolph's first lieutenant at the AFL-CIO, said that Randolph's charisma made him a favorite among unionists and progressives. Randolph had taken so much abuse from the government

A. Philip Randolph. *Courtesy of State Archives of Florida, Florida Memory.*

that "when he called [activists] to do anything, they turned out," Rustin remembered. "Many times up there we had Randolph's auditorium jammed with black trade unionists [and] church leaders in support of 1199. It was a kind of crusade."[140] Randolph asked Rustin to create leaflets in English and Spanish designed at winning support within the black and Hispanic communities for the hospital workers on strike. While 1199 was rallying support for the hospital strike, Randolph's office was also assembling hundreds of young people to go to the March on Washington the following year. "It was a very simple thing to put people on fire about one thing and to divert them to another thing where there was injustice and very obvious injustice to black people," Rustin said.[141] The NAACP, Urban League and Congress of Racial Equality brought additional ground troops to swell the ranks of 1199's picket lines. In short, months before the 1963 March on Washington, Rustin had been mobilizing support for the 1962 strike at Beth-El Hospital in Brooklyn and Manhattan Eye, Ear and Throat Institute.

Randolph also linked up with Puerto Rican–born politician Joseph Monserrat, who had constructed a citywide multiethnic coalition of African Americans, West Indians and Puerto Ricans. Born in Bayamón, Puerto Rico, Monserrat was a proxy leader for all Latinos, not just Puerto Ricans, and he held seats on multiple state committees related to labor exploitation and civil rights. By the time Randolph asked him to help organize the hospital workers' conference, Monserrat had become a power broker among Latinos.[142]

EMERGENCY ACTION CONFERENCE, 1962

On June 29, 1962, about 150 people met at 217 West 125th Street in Harlem to discuss the hospital workers' ongoing labor dispute. William K. De Fossett, an undercover FBI detective, attended the conference and wrote a detailed report describing the people who attended the conference and what they said. FBI surveillance records and 1199 correspondence show that a large number of the city's black and Hispanic leaders attended the conference, including noted intellectuals, performers, community activists and unionists. Some of those in attendance were author James Baldwin; actor Ossie Davis; radical Puerto Rican labor organizer and politician Gilberto Gerena Valentín; Jamaican-born labor organizer and future leader of the Negro American Labor Council Cleveland Robinson, who was the vice-president of District 65 Distributive Workers of America, an advisor to Dr. King and chairman of the 1963 March on Washington; African American attorney Cora Walker, the first female president of the Harlem Lawyers Association; and folk singer Pete Seeger.[143]

De Fossett's report confirmed that black and Hispanic leaders collaborated extensively to promote the civil rights and labor movements. In that regard, the participation of Malcolm X at the conference is remarkable. It was the first time that Malcolm X backed a labor union and the first time as Elijah Muhammad's representative for the Nation of Islam that he joined a multiethnic coalition. In 1962, Malcolm X was at

From left to right: Pete Seeger, Ossie Davie and Ruby Dee Singing at a 1199 Event. *Courtesy of Kheel Center, Cornell University.*

the height of his popularity.[144] According to the FBI report, Malcolm X sat silently during much of the discussion and listened to the comments of other activists. Davis, the head of 1199, said, "We talk so much about the conditions in the South…we forget about the conditions in our own backyard. It is no accident that ninety-five percent of the hospital workers were black and Puerto Rican—no one else would take such a low-paying and degrading job." Davis also condemned Congressman Powell for not taking a more active role in the labor dispute.[145] Percy Sutton, a prominent Harlem-based activist, owner of the *New York Amsterdam News* and WLIB radio station and future Manhattan borough president, threw his support behind the hospital workers. Sutton proposed that the leaders of the different community organizations represented at the conference join the picket line. "We can't have civil rights until Negroes and Puerto Ricans have human rights."[146] Monserrat argued a similar point. He thought the city's white, privileged elites needed to learn that the city would not function "without the low-income workers. If all of these people would stop working for one day," he added, "the city would be at a standstill."[147] When Malcolm X spoke, he compared the problem of African Americans and Puerto Ricans in New York City with the problems of Blacks and Mexicans in Los Angeles. He severely criticized black ministers and community leaders for failing the people they should have helped. Malcolm X offered all of the community leaders and clergy the opportunity to speak at an upcoming Muslim rally in New York in July. "If the Negro and Puerto Rican are the balance of power in this city," he stated, "then they should use it and demand that the city government take action in this labor dispute."[148] At the conclusion of the meeting, Rustin declared that a committee co-chaired by Randolph and Monserrat would be formed to increase community support for the hospital workers. This group was later named the Committee for Justice to Hospital Workers (CJHW).[149]

CJHW set up a committee to raise money and collect food for the strikers.[150] The list of vice-chairmen included James Baldwin, Ossie Davis, James Farmer, Louis Hernandez, Juan Mas, Frieda Montaldo, Cleveland Robinson, Percy Sutton, Gilberto Gerena Valentín and Cora Walker. Rustin served as the executive secretary.[151] News of the creation of the CJHW had its projected result. Days after, Governor Nelson Rockefeller brought both sides to the negotiation table and publicly pledged to introduce legislation giving voluntary hospital workers coverage under the state labor relations act and to back local legislation giving collective bargaining rights to workers at voluntary hospitals in the next legislative session. As a result, organizers

Malcolm X speaks at a rally in support of black and Puerto Rican 1199 workers. *Courtesy of Kheel Center, Cornell University.*

suspended the second strike on July 18, 1962, and the CJHW planned a prayer pilgrimage on July 22, 1962.[152] The goals of the event seemed to be to celebrate the end of the strike and apply political pressure on the governor so that he would keep his commitment in the months to come.[153]

An incomplete speakers list at the prayer pilgrimage included Malcolm X; Martin Luther King Jr.; Roy Wilkins, the national executive secretary of the NAACP; Harry Van Arsdale; Leon Davis; Monserrat Flores, president of the United Puerto Rican Organizations of the Bronx; Max Gonzalez, president of the Council of Puerto Rican and Spanish-American Organizations of New York; Cleveland Robinson; Percy Sutton; Gilberto Gerena Valentín; Celia Vice, vice-president of the Council of Puerto Rican Organizations of Brooklyn; and Joseph Monserrat. Police estimates put the crowd at more than 2,300 people—blacks, whites and Hispanics.

We know that Malcolm X came, but Martin Luther King Jr. did not. Malcolm X addressed the crowd in his distinctively fast and forceful tempo. His words reflected both his empathy with the workers and his respect for Davis:

> *For the conditions that exist, it is important for our people, for the Puerto Ricans and the so-called Negroes…the masses of the people who are workers want a solution to their problems. Don't select anybody to speak for you who is compromising or who is afraid of upsetting the status quo or the apple cart of those people who are running City Hall or sitting in Albany or sitting in the White House. As Leon Davis has already proven, you don't get a job done unless you show the man that you're not afraid to go to jail. If you aren't willing to pay that price then you don't need the rewards or the benefits that go along with it.*[154]

The CJHW had scheduled Dr. King to follow Malcolm X, but "conditions in Albany, Georgia made it impossible" for him to attend.[155] In his absence, he sent an audiotape message of support that CJHW played to the crowd:

> *It was my sincere hope to be able to address the prayer pilgrimage because of my deep conviction that the struggle for justice, freedom, and dignity in New York City is part and parcel of the fight we are waging today in Albany, Georgia....The full implications of Local 1199's historic victory will have a profound effect upon millions of unorganized workers throughout the nation....I want to extend my very hearty congratulations to Mr. Randolph and Mr. Monserrat for their effective leadership of the Committee for Justice to hospital workers. Your demonstration of unity of all sections of the Negro and Puerto Rican communities was decisive in achieving a victorious settlement. That unity spells even greater victories in the immediate future....I am convinced that whatever differences we have in approaching [problems] should be and can be clarified within our community, and that regardless of our differences we must present a show of unity in regard to the solution of these vital problems. If this cannot be achieved, it is clear to me that the opposition will utilize our inability to cooperate to divide us and to weaken that degree of unity which is imperative if we are to achieve justice and freedom in our time.*[156]

In the end, the organizing efforts of 1199, the resolve of the workers and the formation of the CJHW compelled Governor Rockefeller's mediation and the eventual settlement of the strike.[157] The CJHW kept up the pressure until the state legislature passed laws in 1965 granting unions the right to represent hospital workers in the state. By 1968, it had negotiated a doubling of the salaries for hospital workers.[158] Randolph and Monserrat, similar to King, saw the hospital workers' strike as part of the larger fight of blacks and Latinos in the city. "The unshakeable unity of the Negro and Puerto Rican communities, forged in the struggle for justice for the hospital workers, must be continued and expanded," said one CJHW resolution. "This fight involves more than the hospital workers. It is part of the larger fight in our city against discrimination and exploitation, against slums, against juvenile delinquency, against drug addiction, against all forms of degradation that result from poverty and human misery."[159]

At the end of the strike, the leadership of the CJHW wrote, "Our united effort in the interests of the hospital workers has taught us an old but decisive lesson—that in unity there is strength. We hereby pledge to continue the work of our committee to win first-class citizenship rights, human dignity and human rights—right here and right now."[160]

WHERE PEOPLE WENT TO EAT, MEET, REST, PLAN AND STRATEGIZE

NEW ORLEANS, LOUISIANA, 1959–1960s: DOOKY CHASE'S RESTAURANT

With $600 borrowed from a local beer company, jazz musician Edgar "Dooky" Chase started Dooky Chase's Restaurant in the historic Treme neighborhood of New Orleans in 1936 during the Depression. Since its opening, it has been a fixture in black New Orleans, making traditional and Creole-style soul food dishes. The original location could be described as nothing more than a street corner stand that sold lottery tickets and po' boy sandwiches. By 1941, Dooky Chase's became a local bar and grill selling typical down-home New Orleans food across the street from its original corner sandwich stand location. Edgar Chase spent more time working on his professional musical career while his wife and later his son, Edgar "Dooky" Chase Jr., helped grow the business.[161]

In 1946, Edgar "Dooky" Chase Jr. married Leah Chase, a native of Madison, Louisiana, who was steeped in the culinary culture of the "Creole de Couleur." It was Leah Chase, later known as the "Queen of Creole Cuisine," who infused the family-owned and operated restaurant with a Creole flavor. To the original menu, she added her own family recipes and other recipes she gained from her time working in French Quarter restaurants, attracting patrons of all colors despite Jim Crow laws. "I'd worked in some of the finest restaurants in the French Quarter and wanted the same thing for my people, in my neighborhood," she recalled. "I had one dream: to make this a truly fine restaurant for black people and to raise the standards of the whole community."[162] Dooky Chase's Restaurant would become just that—and more.

An Eating and Meeting Place for Activists

Until the late 1960s and early 1970s, New Orleans had been a city that the white power structure kept segregated. African Americans made up 40 percent of the city's population but could not shop or eat in many places. Canal Street served as the main shopping district, but white store owners operated rigidly segregated businesses that sold black folks goods but would not seat them at their lunch counters or let them use their segregated bathrooms. In the city's black shopping districts on Dryades Street, white Jewish merchants operated stores that were open to blacks but refused to employ them above the rank of custodians. The Crescent City began to change as Japanese forces attacked Pearl Harbor on December 7, 1941. The next day, the U.S. government declared war on the Japanese, and subsequently, Germany and Italy, allies of the Japanese, declared war on the United States. FDR sought to mobilize popular support for U.S. entry in World War II, calling for victory against fascism in Europe and Asia. In response, African Americans called for support for a Double V campaign: victory against antidemocratic forces abroad and at home.

In the winter of 1941, the People's Defense League (PDL), a New Orleans–based voter registration and education group, organized the first and largest voter registration initiative in New Orleans since the end of Reconstruction. The initiative included protest against white city officials in charge of elections who sought to block the registration of would-be black voters. PDL protest toward that effort included some five hundred people. Ernest J. Wright, the promotional director, told newspaper reporters that the PDL had spent several weeks organizing the protest in predominantly African American wards in New Orleans. Reverend A.L. Davis also participated in the voter registration drive. The voter registration drive and protest slowly provided Democratic openings in the Crescent City. By 1944, African Americans in New Orleans voted without opposition or intimidation in the September 12 Democratic primary in Louisiana. Following the primary members of the Louisiana Association for the Progress of Negro Citizens and the People's Defense League organized a house-to-house voter registration drive for the upcoming presidential election.[163]

WHERE PEOPLE WENT TO EAT, MEET, REST, PLAN AND STRATEGIZE

CIO labor leader and PDL commissioner Ernest J. Wright had been most active in registering and educating potential voters in Louisiana's Eleventh and Twelfth Wards, which had a concentration of African American residents. Wright served as one of the most militant African American labor leaders in the Crescent City in the late 1940s. Reverend Davis, president of the Louisiana Association for the Progress of Negro Citizens, worked closely with Wright in registering and educating black voters in New Orleans. In 1944, African American voters participated in a Louisiana primary in large numbers analogous to how they had turned out on election days during the Reconstruction period.[164] In preparation for the 1944 general election for president, Wright helped organize a CIO-sponsored voter mobilization mass meeting; the PDL held a similar event the same day. The meeting provided the opportunity for the audience to hear the platform of each of the candidates. A straw poll taken at the gathering revealed that African Americans overwhelmingly supported FDR. Black voters in New Orleans had historically been registered Republicans. African Americans voted in the largest numbers in the Seventh, Tenth, Eleventh and Twelfth Wards; all but the Seventh Ward went for Roosevelt. Several years later Wright and the PDL would go on to launch a movement similar to that which the New Negro Alliance had done in Washington, D.C., in the 1930s and 1940s. The PDL and their coalition partners, including Reverend Davis, organized the Consumers' League of Greater New Orleans (CLGNO) in the 1950s to end segregation and fight for job opportunities for blacks.[165]

A Celebrity Hot Spot

For decades, Dooky Chase's served prominent African American politicians, musicians and businesspeople. This was the place people like Ray Charles—who wrote "Early in the Mornin'" about it—would come after local shows, staying up until the wee hours telling stories and eating gumbo, some of the city's best.[166] In 1954, a newspaper reporter described Dooky Chase's as New Orleans's leading African American restaurant and bar. "Located at 2301 Orleans in the Creole section of town, the Dooky Chase restaurant bar is the meeting place for the locals and out-of-towners."[167] In addition to Ray Charles, the restaurant also served noted African American entertainers, such as Count Basie, Sarah Vaughan, Lena Horne, Duke Ellington and Cab Calloway, all of whom came to play for white patrons in New Orleans's segregated venues, where Jim Crow laws prohibited them from eating. "There was no other place to go, really," recalled Leah Chase, so word of mouth led them to Dooky Chase's.[168]

At the same time, activists met at Dooky Chase's and other spaces to organize a new phase of the civil rights struggle in New Orleans. Activists in the 1950s and '60s were waging the battle to end segregation in city eateries and employment discrimination among merchants on Dryades and Rampart Streets, which depended on African American customers yet refused to employ them as store clerks.[169] It was from Dooky Chase's that members of the CLGNO organized the new phase of the movement over gumbo. The restaurant was one of the only spaces in New Orleans where black and white activists could meet to plan their progressive movements during the civil rights movement. "It was a meeting place, and if a person needed to see someone in the black community, they'd come here, because this was where everyone met," recalled Leah Chase.[170] Although public officials viewed these gatherings as a violation of Jim Crow laws, Dooky Chase's proved too popular to close down without the possibility of causing serious resistance from its white patrons and the residents of Treme.

DOOKY'S CREOLE GUMBO

Serves 8 to 10

4 hard-shell crabs, cleaned
½ pound Creole hot sausage, cut into bite-size pieces
½ pound smoked sausage, cut into bite-size pieces
½ pound beef, cubed
½ pound smoked ham, cubed
½ cup peanut oil
4 tablespoons flour
1 cup onions, chopped
3 quarts water
6 chicken wings, cut in half
1 pound shrimp, peeled and deveined
1 tablespoon paprika
1 tablespoon salt
1 tablespoon file powder
2 dozen oysters, with liquid

¼ cup chopped parsley
3 cloves garlic, minced
1 teaspoon ground thyme

Put crabs, sausages, stew meat and ham in a 5-quart pot over a medium flame. Cover and cook in its own fat for 25 minutes. Heat oil in skillet and add flour to make a roux. Brown until golden. Add onions and cook over low heat until onions wilt. Pour onion mixture over the ingredients in a large pot. Add water, chicken wings, shrimp, paprika, salt and file powder. Bring to a boil and cook for 30 minutes. Add oysters, parsley, garlic and thyme. Lower heat and cook for 10 minutes more. Serve over rice.

Modified from the Los Angeles Sentinel, *February 10, 1999*

CAJUN RICE

Serves 4 to 6

1 can giblet gravy
1 can condensed tomato soup
1 soup can water
3 cups instant rice
2 tablespoons instant minced onion
¼ teaspoon hot pepper sauce
½ cup diced cooked ham or chicken
½ cup sliced hot Spanish or Italian sausage

Combine the first six ingredients. Bring to a boil on top of the stove. Add ham or chicken and sliced sausage. Place in buttered casserole and set in a moderately hot oven (375 degrees Fahrenheit) for about 15 minutes.

Modified from the Chicago Daily Defender, *May 3, 1966*

NEW ORLEANS GRITS PUDDING
Serves 6

4 cups milk
½ cup sugar
½ teaspoon salt
½ cup raisins
⅛ teaspoon cinnamon
1 tablespoon grated orange peel
½ cup white hominy grits
1½ teaspoons unflavored gelatin
¼ cup cold water
1 teaspoon vanilla

Begin by combining milk, sugar, salt, raisins, cinnamon and orange peel in saucepan. Bring to a boil. Slowly stir in grits. Reduce heat; cover and cook about 25 minutes, stirring frequently. Soften gelatin in cold water. Add softened gelatin and vanilla to grits mixture; stir until gelatin is dissolved. Remove from heat. Pour into a 1-quart mold that has been rinsed with cold water. Chill until firm. To serve, unmold; garnish with drained whole kumquats or kumquat flowers and clear orange sauce (optional).

Modified from the Philadelphia Tribune, *Mar 23, 1968*

Protests and Sit-Ins

Raphael Cassimere Jr. was a student at the University of New Orleans in 1960. He joined the newly established NAACP Youth Council in July 1960. He participated in "the first sit-ins at lunch counters against F.W. Woolworth and some other stores. This was in September of 1960." Cassimere said that "most of the people" who initially participated in the movement had attended his high school. "Some of us had been friends before, so obviously we all knew each other very well." According to Cassimere, the movement mobilized diverse groups of protesters and supporters.[171]

WHERE PEOPLE WENT TO EAT, MEET, REST, PLAN AND STRATEGIZE

He and other college students in New Orleans would "picket during their off-hours while they would work fulltime as students." In addition to college students, the sit-in movement in New Orleans had mobilized "high school students, junior high students, and even a few elementary school students," said Cassimere, who describes it as "a youth-led movement."[172]

He also recalled that many whites picketed alongside African American protesters. Other white supporters gave financial and legal aid to the movement. In addition to the movement's racial diversity, he noted that the protesters had religious diversity among them. Cassimere described the movement in New Orleans as an "ecumenical movement" involving Christians, Jews and "a few Muslims at that time."[173]

During protests, police arrested protesters picketing at Walgreens, Winn-Dixie and the TG&Y dime store. The demonstration included members of the Congress for Racial Equality (CORE), the NAACP and the sponsoring organization for the protest, the CLGNO. A crowd of nearly three hundred gathered nearby to cheer on five arrested men despite warnings from New Orleans mayor DeLesseps Morrison that police would arrest anyone involved in public protest. The September 1960 protest served as the first such demonstration in the city. CLGNO leader Henry R. Mitchell, thirty-nine at the time, said that his organization and its supporters would "fill up the jail" before they stopped demonstrating against racist hiring practices in a shopping district in which black folks represented 90 percent of the store customers. He went on to say they had a "good supply" of reserves on hand to take the place of those arrested. Protesters on the picket line carried signs that read, "Don't buy where you can't work" and "First-Class Dollars for First-Class Jobs."[174]

New Orleans police arrested Sydney L. Goldfinch, a twenty-one-year-old male Tulane University undergraduate student, charging him with criminal anarchy, criminal mischief and disturbing the peace. The anarchy charge carried a maximum penalty of ten years in prison. Police arrested Goldfinch four days after he had participated in an integrated sit-in movement at a McCrory's store lunch counter with three African American students—twenty-two-year-old Cecil Carter, twenty-one-year-old Rudolph Lombard and twenty-one-year-old Aretha Kassel—in downtown New Orleans on September 17, 1960. The students said they came to end segregated lunch counters or get arrested. Newspapers reported that lunch counter arrests brought the number of persons picked up in a twenty-four-hour period for sit-ins and picketing a neighborhood shopping center to ten. During the course of the demonstration, as many as 1,500 people marched around the shopping center to protest against racist hiring practices of stores in the center. CLGNO's Reverend A.L. Davis, secretary, and Reverend Avery Alexander, vice-chairman, led the march. Alexander told reporters that his organization's next plan was a political education campaign about why African American people should not spend their money at businesses that refused to hire them.[175]

Almost a year later, the CLGNO threatened to boycott New Orleans Public Service (NOPS), which operated public buses and streetcars in Greater New Orleans, if it didn't provide equal job opportunities for African Americans. In 1958, the CLGNO had forced the company to end its race-based preferential seating policies for white customers on buses and streetcars. In 1961, NOPS hired its first two African American bus drivers to avoid the boycott.[176]

In November 1961, the CLGNO asked the NOPS to hire African American as meter readers and for other positions within the company. If the company failed to do so, the CLGNO threatened to launch a boycott against streetcars, buses and the city's electricity and gas companies. The company agreed to the hiring as soon as it could find the right people. CLGNO also started a "buy where you work" campaign and boycott against stores in the Dryades Street area. The boycott resulted in the closure of one large department store in the area.

The CLGNO carried out boycotts in other areas of New Orleans as well. In December 1961, New Orleans police officials arrested CLGNO president Avery Alexander and vice-president Carlton J. Roy Sr. for marching in protest against the Orleans Parish voter registrar for practicing anti–African American discrimination. City officials refused to grant the organization a permit to hold a public demonstration against the registrar. As a result, members of the CLGNO went forward with the non-permitted demonstration, resulting in the police arresting 303 protesters. Reverend Davis, president of the Louisiana Association for the Progress and Secretary of the CLGNO, led 7,000 protesters as they marched around city hall calling for school desegregation, equal access to public accommodations and equal job opportunities in New Orleans.[177]

In October 1963, the CLGNO mobilized ten thousand African Americans to attend an Orleans Parish County school board meeting protesting the enforcement of a 1960 court decision ending school segregation in the Crescent City. At a CLGNO organized mass meeting, Reverend Avery Alexander told the crowd, "We will need 5000 maybe 10,000 of you" to support the organization's PTA Council, which had produced a petition demanding the school board take necessary steps to ensure the creation of one educational system for all "children, teachers, and other personnel" in Orleans Parish.[178] The courts called for the desegregation of the school system through the fifth grade. By 1963, the implementation had not occurred, leading to the CLGNO massive mobilization effort at the fall 1963 school board meeting.[179]

In November 1963, activists in Louisiana filed an eighteen-point antidiscrimination petition to the mayor of New Orleans Victor Schiro at his city hall office. Members of CORE, the New Orleans Ministerial Alliance and CLGNO participated in the action. The petition, which the mayor rejected, included the demand for equal treatment in city hall, including desegregating its cafeteria. Police dragged CLGNO president Avery Alexander out of the cafeteria by his heels as he protested its Jim Crow policy of not serving blacks. Thirty protestors delivered the petition to the mayor that demanded the repeal of school desegregation and insisted on equal access to public accommodations and equal job opportunities. The protestors stated that they would sit in at city hall until they received a response to the petition.[180]

The Queen of Creole Cuisine

In the 1960s, Dooky Chase's continued to feed leaders and rank-and-file members of the civil rights revolution. Leah Chase recalled that she "fed civil rights workers when they would come in…to the restaurant, and we made this big pot of gumbo. We cooked; they ate; they planned, then they went on."[181]

Speaking about Dooky Chase's, one reporter wrote in 1965, "The food is superlative especially the soft-shell crabs, fried crisp and the stuffed crabs on toast, shrimp creole, and stuffed jumbo shrimp. The latter could double for baby lobsters any time—they're that big!"[182] The civil rights movement in New Orleans came of age in the early 1940s just as the restaurant had transformed from a typical community bar and grill to one of the only African American–owned upscale restaurants in the Crescent City. Ten years into the civil rights movement in the city, the restaurant had gained a reputation as an important meeting space for activists, politicians and social movement leaders. It also gained a reputation for Leah Chase's Creole cuisine. Folks raved about many of the Creole dishes on the restaurant's menu, including its excellent chicken sausage jambalaya. Leah Chase's nickname, Queen of

Creole Cuisine, was well-deserved, and her classic Creole food was gloriously influenced by the city's French, Sicilian and Italian traditions. Folks still rave about Chase's crab bisque even to this day. "The crab bisque was heavenly," recalled one recent patron.[183] "This is the place to order any Southern favorite," another said. "Stewed okra, filé gumbo, and sweet potatoes, for instance, are all prepared in traditional Creole style. Don't expect the usual greasiness that accompanies most Southern food."[184]

CHICKEN AND SAUSAGE JAMBALAYA

Serves 8

4 slices bacon, chopped
1½ cups sliced celery
1 cup rice
1 cup chopped onion
1 cup chopped green pepper
1 16-ounce can tomatoes
½ pound Louisiana sausage, cut in ½-inch pieces
1½ cups water
½ cup garlic-flavored barbecue sauce
1 teaspoon salt
⅛ teaspoon ground red pepper
1½ cups chopped chicken, cooked

Fry bacon until crisp in 3-quart Dutch oven or large frying pan. Stir in celery, rice, onion and green pepper; cook for 5 minutes, stirring frequently. Add tomatoes, sausage, water, barbecue sauce and seasonings. Mix well. Bring to boil. Reduce heat, cover and simmer for 20 minutes. Stir occasionally. Add chicken. Cook 5 minutes longer. Remove from heat and serve.

Los Angeles Sentinel February 10, 1999

WHERE PEOPLE WENT TO EAT, MEET, REST, PLAN AND STRATEGIZE

Accomplishments in New Orleans

Raphael Cassimere Jr. reflected on the civil rights movement of the 1960s in New Orleans, saying, "We didn't get very much done the first year, but at least we got organized and it led to much bigger actions over the next four or five years," including desegregating "all of the cafeterias and the lunch counters," getting stores to hire African Americans as more than cooks and janitors and gaining hundreds of people employment opportunities in places that had never hired African Americans before.[185] In New Orleans, protesters built on the work of students in Atlanta who had forced the two parties' 1960 presidential candidates to talk about race relations during the campaign. Those who had participated in the New Orleans sit-in movement went on to participate in a well-organized voter registration drive in the city during the 1960 presidential election between John F. Kennedy and Richard Nixon. In that election, African Americans provided the small margin of victory that Kennedy needed to defeat Nixon and take the White House from Republicans.

ATLANTA, GEORGIA, 1960: PASCHAL'S RESTAURANT

Brothers James and Robert Paschal first opened a thirty-seat lunch counter sandwich shop on Hunter Street in Atlanta, Georgia, in 1947. Over time, they moved to a location adjacent to the Atlanta University Center (AUC) and expanded their business to include a motel, a nightclub on the famous Chitlin' Circuit and an upscale restaurant. In 1960, the AUC consisted of Morehouse (all male), Spelman (all female), Clark (coed) and Morris Brown (coed) colleges; the Interdenominational Theological Center (all male), a seminary; and Atlanta University (coed), which included a graduate school. The collective student body of the six schools totaled about four thousand. The AUC resided in the middle of an African American community in southwest Atlanta where fear of blacks generally kept whites out of the neighborhood. Atlanta city officials gave Paschal's a "colored only" Jim Crow restaurant seating designation. However, the restaurant's famed fried chicken and other menu items attracted white diners, who made up some 70 percent of its regular customers. The brothers had committed to employ as many AUC college students as they could, knowing that many of them

James Paschal. *Courtesy of the Atlanta History Center.*

needed the money. Many of their student employees went on to join the sit-in movement in Atlanta.[186]

According to Marcellas C.D. Barksdale, who attended Morehouse in the early 1960s, Paschal's was no dump. To the contrary, it was a white tablecloth restaurant for middle- and upper-class African Americans in Atlanta. He said that it was the "number-one so-called classy restaurant" for African American professionals. During segregation, it remained the first choice for a Sunday meal for "Doctor and Mrs. So-and-So." In addition, well-to-do Morehouse students would also take their "public girlfriends" to Paschal's for Sunday dinner, said Barksdale. You could get full-course, great-tasting meals for two people for five dollars. In addition to formal dining, Pashcal's also had a lunch counter and grill, where you could order fried chicken, collards, cornbread and biscuits in a casual setting.[187]

In 1934, the *Atlanta Daily World* published a number of recipes. In the introduction to the recipes, the food editor, whose name remains unknown, wrote:

> *Through the courtesy of the Municipal Market, the Atlanta Daily World is able to pass on to its many readers some very excellent recipes. These recipes are "tried and true" recipes which have been thoroughly tested by the Georgia State Department of Agriculture....World readers are*

always advised by state leaders to use, as far as possible, Georgia grown and made products in their cooking. "Use Georgia Products and Help Georgia" is the motto.[188]

GEORGIA PECAN PRALINES

1 cup milk
2 cups sugar
1 to 2 cups caramelized sugar
⅓ stick butter
2 cups pecan halves

Mix milk and sugar. Add caramelized sugar. Boil to soft ball stage. Remove from heat. Add butter and beat until ready to sugar. Mix in pecan halves. Drop on oiled paper.

Modified from the Atlanta Daily World, *June 30, 1934*

GEORGIA PEACH PIE

Yields 1 9-inch pie

2 pie pastry crusts
4 cups sliced fresh peaches
½ cup sugar
1 tablespoon flour

Line pie pan with pastry. Arrange peaches in pie shell and sift sugar and flour over them. Place strips of pastry lattice fashion over top of pie and bake in moderately hot oven (400 degrees Fahrenheit) for 30 minutes. Reduce to 375 degrees and continue baking for thirty more minutes, or until brown and peaches are done.

Modified from the Pittsburgh Courier, *August 30, 1941*

Access to recipes directly from Paschal's could not be obtained. However, Atlanta-born chef Bob Jeffries provided some insights into a similar style of cooking. He says cooking southern style, or what some people call soul food, is cooking with what you have on hand and knowing how to season it to make it taste good.[189] In the late 1960s, Jeffries worked as a chef at Daly's Dandelion, a one-time saloon on Third Avenue at Sixty-First Street in New York City. The *Chicago Defender*'s food writer Poppy Cannon described it as a hot spot for a Sunday brunch in New York City. The *Defender* published a number of Jeffries's old Atlanta recipes reminiscent of the food served at Paschal's.[190]

COLLARD GREENS
Serves 6

2 packages frozen collard greens
1 tablespoon minced instant onion
1 small hot chili pepper
2 slices thick-cut country-style bacon (and reserved bacon fat)

(Bob Jeffries cooks fresh collard greens with ham hocks, adding plenty of onion and hot pepper. You could, however, settle for frozen.)

Cook frozen collard greens according to directions, adding minced onion and hot chili pepper. Meanwhile, fry slices of bacon. Reserve the fat. Add 2 tablespoons of the bacon fat to the cooked, drained collard greens. Sprinkle the crumbled bacon on top. A cruet of hot pepper sauce should be on hand for the real southerners.

Modified from the Chicago Daily Defender, *February 22, 1968*

BOB JEFFRIES'S FABULOUS PECAN PIE

2 well-beaten eggs
1 cup dark corn syrup
1 cup white sugar
1 cup broken-up pecan pieces
2 tablespoons butter
1 teaspoon vanilla
¼ teaspoon salt
1 8- or 9-inch pie shell

WHERE PEOPLE WENT TO EAT, MEET, REST, PLAN AND STRATEGIZE

Combine well-beaten eggs with dark corn syrup, white sugar and pecan pieces. Add butter, vanilla and salt. Pour mixture in a baked pie shell. Bake in a moderately hot oven (375 degrees Fahrenheit) about 25 minutes. This pie is very rich, so you need serve only a small wedge, with or without whipped, sour or ice cream.

Modified from the Chicago Daily Defender, *February 22, 1968*

GEORGIA FRIED CHICKEN

"Mrs. Dull and her book, Southern Cooking, are considered in many quarters of the South as the ultimate authority. Henrietta Stanley Dull was born shortly after the close of the War between the States and lived to be 100 years old.... Although she was adept at all sorts of elegant cookery, Mrs. Dull's greatest claim to fame are her careful, clear and explicit directions for preparing celestial versions of simple dishes, like her never-to-be-forgotten fried chicken."[191]
—Poppy Cannon, food writer, *Chicago Daily Defender*

1 young chicken, weighing from 1½ to 2 pounds
vegetable shortening
1½ to 2 cups flour
salt and pepper

Prepare a small chicken or use a cut-up frying chicken. Have a deep-fry pan ready with shortening at least 2 inches deep (Lard was often used, or in later years, vegetable shortening.)
  Sift enough flour in which to roll the chicken pieces. Add salt and pepper to the flour and roll each chicken piece in flour. Place in hot grease. Put the largest pieces in first and on the hottest part of the pan. Cover for 5 min. Remove cover and turn when underside is well browned. Replace cover for another 5 min., and then cook in open pan until bottom side is brown, about 30 minutes if chicken is not too large. Do not turn but once; too much turning and too long cooking will destroy the fine flavor.

Modified from the Chicago Daily Defender, *February 12, 1968*

PICKLED BEETS

5 large beets, sliced or diced
½ cup vinegar
½ cup sugar
1 teaspoon clove spice

Put all ingredients into a quart of water and let cook slowly for about 45 minutes.

Modified from the Chicago Daily Defender, *May 9, 1963*

CORNBREAD

2 cups cornmeal
½ cup flour
2 teaspoons baking powder
1 teaspoon sugar
pinch salt
1½ cups buttermilk
2 eggs
1 tablespoon shortening

Sift together all dry ingredients. Add buttermilk, stirring constantly. Add whole eggs, again stirring constantly. Melt shortening and add to mixture, stirring until smooth. Preheat oven to 400 degrees Fahrenheit. Either place the mixture into muffin tin or flat pan. Let cook for 30 minutes.

Modified from the Chicago Daily Defender, *May 9, 1963*

SWEET POTATO PONE

5 large, firm sweet potatoes
3 cups sweet milk
2½ cups sugar
6 eggs
¼ pound butter

WHERE PEOPLE WENT TO EAT, MEET, REST, PLAN AND STRATEGIZE

1 teaspoon nutmeg
½ teaspoon vanilla flavoring
½ teaspoon baking powder
½ cup flour

Boil potatoes for 30 minutes. Once they are cool enough, peel and mash thoroughly, making sure no lumps remain. Let cool and add milk, stirring constantly. Add remaining ingredients and mix well. Preheat oven to 350 degrees Fahrenheit. Place mixture in Pyrex dish and let cook for about 1 hour, or until golden-brown glaze is achieved.

Modified from the Chicago Daily Defender, *May 9, 1963*

An Eating and Meeting Place for Activists

Like Georgia Gilmore's business in Montgomery, Paschal's Restaurant played an important role during the civil rights movement. It, too, literally fed the rank and file of the civil rights revolution and its leaders with sensational soul food, providing a popular meeting place for activists. After the success of the Montgomery Improvement Association (MIA) and the end of the Jim Crow laws on buses in Montgomery, Martin Luther King returned to Atlanta, where he organized the Southern Christian Leadership Conference (SCLC) and served as associate pastor of Ebenezer Baptist Church, his father's church. Upon his return to Atlanta, King asked the Paschals for permission to "bring his team members and guest to Paschal's to eat, meet, rest, plan, and strategize."

"How could we refuse? We had the resources and the place," said James Paschal.[192] The brothers viewed the request as a calling from God to support the movement. Thereafter, civil rights groups, such as NAACP and CORE, held organizing meetings in the restaurant, where they "feast[ed] on Robert's fried chicken." James Paschal said some activists and organizations "called Paschal's either their first or second home." Many of these groups had little or no money, so the Paschal brothers organized and sponsored luncheons and dinners and provided hotel and meeting rooms. "Those who could pay did so," but the Paschals "never said no." For MLK and his team, they set aside a meeting room where they planned civil rights events like the March on Washington and Mississippi Freedom Summer.[193]

The interior of Paschal's Restaurant, 831 West Hunter Street, Atlanta. *Courtesy of the* Atlanta *Journal Constitution.*

"QUILLY":
A SPECIAL VERSION OF A
SOUTHERN CHARLOTTE

"When Dr. Martin Luther King Jr. came back home to Atlanta from Sweden some years ago with the Nobel Peace Prize, what did he want to eat? According to his mother, Mrs. King Sr., she explained that "Quilly," a cool gentle dessert is necessary after the King's [sic] favorite supper of ribs, collard greens, and baked sweet potatoes. Quilly, according to Mrs. King Sr., was the name the children had given this dessert years ago. She speculates that "maybe [it was] because it was garnished with spikes of thin sugar wafers."[194]
—Poppy Cannon, food writer, *Chicago Daily Defender*

Serves 8

1 tablespoon gelatin
¼ cup cold water
¼ cup boiling water
1 cup sugar
1 pint heavy cream, whipped
¼ pound chopped almonds
6 stale macaroons, crumbled
1 dozen marshmallows
1 can fruit salad, well drained
1 teaspoon vanilla or rum extract

Soak gelatin in cold water for 5 minutes. Then dissolve in boiling water. Add sugar. When mixture is cool, add the whipped heavy cream, chopped almonds, stale macaroon crumbles, marshmallows and fruit salad. Flavor with vanilla or rum extract. Pour into a quart mold that has been rinsed in cold water. At serving time, decorate with sugar wafers.

Modified from the Chicago Daily Defender, *December 12, 1967*

Lonnie King

Betty Johnson of Attalla, Alabama, briefly attended North Carolina A&T in the 1950s. Fear of white hostility dissuaded her and her classmates from ever trying to enter white restaurants in downtown Greensboro. Instead, they enjoyed the fried chicken and pork chops available at black-owned Barry's Grill, one of the most popular places in the city's African American community.[195] On February 1, 1960, students Ezell Blair Jr., David Richmond, Joseph McNeil and Franklin McCain from North Carolina A&T participated in sit-ins at the Woolworth's and S.H. Kress store lunch counters to force the businesses to end a segregated eating policy. Morehouse College student Lonnie King read about the Greensboro movement and decided to start a similar one in Atlanta.[196]

Other influences also motivated Lonnie King to action in 1960. King was born and raised in Arlington, Georgia, which he described as located in Deep South Georgia, a place where Jim Crow policy was the law and discrimination commonplace. His grandfather, who raised him in Arlington, served as the first influence on Lonnie King's decision to organize a sit-in movement in Atlanta in February 1960. In the rural South, if a white official in a community knew a black person had been involved with the NAACP in any way at that time it meant almost certain death. His grandfather was a covert member of the NAACP who clandestinely recruited members for the organization as he carried on his duty as an itinerant evangelist. Preaching throughout black communities in South Georgia and North Alabama afforded him the opportunity to recruit members for the NAACP; at the time, it cost about fifty cents to join the organization. "One day, son, this organization is going to get us out of slavery," his grandfather told King. "We are still in slavery. The only difference is that we can go home at night but everything else is about the same." He elaborated that African Americans have no rights that a white person respects, not even "the smallest white child."[197]

King moved to Atlanta at age nine and lived with his mother while he attended Atlanta public schools before going on to attend Morehouse College. He spent one year at Morehouse before spending several years in the navy and then returned to Morehouse in 1957. It's not clear if he enlisted or had been drafted. Speaking of his Morehouse years, King recalled, "I played football and did very well on the football team and got somewhat of a following." He also recalled the influence that then Morehouse president Benjamin E. Mays provided, perhaps the second influence on Lonnie King's decision to organize a sit-in movement in Atlanta in February 1960. Mays was one of the greatest educators of his time because, as an intellectual, he possessed the kind of charisma that made students emulate him. Mays's mantra was "you have a mission if you're a Morehouse man" and "that means that you are part of a group of people who can lead this nation." Mays taught the students at Morehouse that they could lead "as well as anyone else," said King.[198]

Julian Bond, whom King met earlier while standing in line registering for classes at Morehouse one semester, served as King's first recruit. In addition, he recruited Roselyn Pope, who was the president of the Spelman student government association at the time. Other initial members who became the movement's steering committee included Morris Dillard and Albert Benson. At the suggestion of one of six AUC college presidents, the committee went to work drafting a manifesto that stated its objectives. After its completion, the organizing members sent it to newspapers. Morehouse and Spelman undergraduates Julian Bond and Herschelle Sullivan wrote the founding document, which King and his cohorts entitled "An Appeal for Human

Right." The document became the movement's adopted name—the Committee on Appeal for Human Rights (COAHR). A successful fundraising effort that netted $12,000 allowed the COAHR to publish its "appeal in all of the newspapers," and an unnamed official read it into the congressional record, King said.[199] The *New York Times* learned about it and reprinted it for free.

Lonnie King, Julian Bond, Herschelle Sullivan, Carolyn Long, Joseph Pierce and other black students from the AUC went into the planning stages, discussing city strategy and how to mobilize students and train them in nonviolence strategy. Many of Paschal's student employees went on to join the sit-in movement in Atlanta. Perhaps the student-employees at Paschal drew the two brothers deeper into the civil rights movement at a time when some black business owners viewed sit-ins as detrimental to their operations. The Paschals supported the transformation of their business into a sanctuary and meeting place for student activists and the unofficial headquarters of the Atlanta civil rights movement. Activists Julian Bond and Lonnie King held strategy meetings at Paschal's, "often right at the table where they were dining," recalled James Paschal. Planning meetings at the restaurant typically started with a prayer and a freedom song. "Robert and I joined in, although neither of us had a voice for singing. We just wanted to be part of helping to break the chains binding us all."[200] The owners' hospitality became key to strategy sessions held in the restaurant, providing activists with needed space to think and weigh their next steps.[201]

In the mid-1960s, soul food took on symbolic meaning in black neighborhoods across the country. Many viewed it as a return to the authentic eating traditions of Africa and the survival skills of the enslaved during the antebellum period. On New Year's Day, for example, African Americans and southerners in general have the tradition of eating black-eyed peas for coins, pork for luck and collard greens for dollars.[202]

BLACK-EYED PEAS

¼ pound bacon or salt pork
1 stalk celery, diced
1 small onion, diced

---

2 packages frozen black-eyed peas
water or consommé
fresh-ground pepper, or 3 drops of hot pepper sauce

Dice bacon or salt pork and fry until crisp. Add celery and onion. Cook until onion is soft. Then add black-eyed peas. Add liquid (water or consommé) and cook as directed on the package. Season with plenty of freshly ground pepper or hot pepper sauce. Serve over or along with cooked rice. Some people combine the rice and black-eyed peas.

Modified from the Chicago Defender, *December 31, 1966*

Next, COAHR organized a series of sit-ins starting on March 9, 1960, at segregated lunch counters in downtown Atlanta, including those at Rich's, Woolworths, S.H. Kress, McCrory's, Grants, two H.L. Green stores, two Walgreens and three Lane stores. The protests continued with most business owners deciding to shut down their lunch counters. Lonnie King noted that, at first, it had been difficult mobilizing AUC students because what they had conceptualized had never been done in Atlanta. However, news of the Greensboro movement and movements in other parts of the country inspired AUC students to join COAHR's Atlanta sit-in movement.

After it started, the movement snowballed, and it became popular on six AUC campuses to participate in the sit-in movement. It became "a matter of keeping up with the Joneses," said King. "We had some students—some who are prominent in Atlanta right now—who refused to participate because they said that they could not be nonviolent. We had to make sure that we had students who were willing to take the blows if necessary in order" for the sit-in to succeed. During demonstrations downtown, Atlanta police arrested ten, twenty and sometimes more AUC students at a time.[203]

The Paschal brothers provided bail money and food for students jailed while protesting Jim Crow laws in Atlanta. The restaurant served as a place where worried parents could pick up children whom state officials had arrested while protesting and then later released on bond.[204] When they made bail, the members of the COAHR went straight to Paschal's, where the restaurant owners would feed them and their families chicken sandwiches and soft drinks for free. When the food was not free at Paschal's

Members of Omega Si Phi Fraternity demonstrate in front of Rich's Department Store in downtown Atlanta. *Courtesy of the Atlanta History Center.*

during the sit-in movements, you could still get a plate of fried chicken, a wedge of corn bread, candied yams and some greens for the price of a poor man's feast—a dollar and some change. "Many times, the bailed-out marchers sat bent over chairs," said James Paschal. "Their heads rested on the table or their tired bodies dropped in heaps on the carpeted floor in various corners of the restaurant."[205] The restaurant's breakfast, lunch or dinner food and desserts would help the demonstrators regain their strength for the next demonstration.

SHRIMP GUMBO

1 green pepper
1 medium-size onion
3 tablespoons butter
3 tablespoons flour
1 teaspoon salt
¼ teaspoon black pepper
1 quart strained tomatoes
2 cups sliced okra
1½ cups cooked shrimp, cut into pieces

Mince green pepper and onion and brown lightly in butter over high heat. Add the flour and seasonings. Gradually, add tomatoes, okra and shrimp. Then reduce to low heat and simmer until the shrimp is tender.

Modified from the Atlanta Daily, *March 20, 1937*

SWEET POTATO CAKE

4 eggs, beaten separately
2 cups sugar
2 cups flour
1 cup mashed sweet potatoes
½ cup sweet milk
¼ cup grated chocolate
1 cup chopped nuts
1 teaspoon ground cinnamon
1 teaspoon ground cloves
1 teaspoon ground allspice
1 teaspoon lemon extract
1 teaspoon vanilla extract
2 teaspoons baking powder

Combine all ingredients. Bake in two layers. Use as filling coconut, chocolate, caramel or plain white icing.

Modified from the Atlanta Daily World, *June 30, 1934*

WHERE PEOPLE WENT TO EAT, MEET, REST, PLAN AND STRATEGIZE

Julian Bond and Marian Wright went to speak with MLK about the need to organize students across the South to advance the civil rights movement. MLK agreed and asked Ella Baker, who served as one of his lieutenants, to organize a meeting. As an alumnae of Shaw University, Baker used her network to have the meeting there. The Student Nonviolent Coordinating Committee (SNCC) emerged out of the Shaw meeting on Easter weekend in 1960. It went on to become the Special Forces troops of the 1960s decade of the civil rights movement in the South.[206]

Protests and a Presidential Influence

Over the summer of 1960, Lonnie King and a core group of student activists within the AUC prepared for a fall protest campaign. They decided to force the candidates running for president in fall of 1960, Democrat John F. Kennedy and Republican Richard N. Nixon, to address the issue of race relations. To accomplish their goal, COAHR decided to focus a sit-in protest on Rich's Department Store, a celebrated southern department store chain based in Atlanta that would later become Macy's. Lonnie King suggested to COAHR's organizing committee that they get MLK to go to jail with its members and that the organizations send telegrams to Nixon and Kennedy "asking them to take a stand on the issue of race" because both campaigns had been ignoring the civil rights struggle in the South.[207] Lonnie King used a phrase from one of MLK's father's sermons to get MLK, who had been on a court-ordered probation from a previous civil disobedience campaign and therefore reluctant to participate in the movement, to allow himself to be arrested. "I told him, 'You can't lead from the back. You gotta lead from the front,'" recalled Lonnie King.[208] The tactic worked, and MLK agreed to participate in a sit-in at the flagship Rich's store in downtown Atlanta. On October 19, King and presidential candidate John F. Kennedy met and discussed the U.S. civil rights movement.

On October 25, 1960, Atlanta police arrested King for violating city segregation laws. MLK refused to post a $500 bond to free himself until going to trial and instead insisted on remaining in jail until the charges against him had been dropped. Picketing in demonstrations expanded to include several hundred to two thousand AUC students at sixteen downtown stores. In response, Atlanta police arrested twenty-six people and a judge sentenced them to "twenty days in the city prison farm, with ten days suspended." Each protestor who made it back from jail safely to Paschal's

Left: Morehouse student Lonnie King (left), unidentified woman and Martin Luther King Jr. during the October 1960 sit-in demonstration protesting lunch counter segregation in Rich's Department Store in downtown Atlanta. *Courtesy of the* Atlanta Journal Constitution.

Below: Police arresting Martin Luther King Jr. and other protestors during an Atlanta sit-in demonstration in October 1960. *Courtesy of the* Atlanta Journal Constitution.

received a hero's welcome, including free food and beverages. "We kept the restaurant open all night when those young people set [*sic*] at the white folks' lunch counters and were refused service," said James Paschal.[209]

Good'N Easy Onion Soup Recipe

12 small white onions
3 tablespoons butter or margarine
1 tablespoon cooking oil
1 teaspoon flour
1 teaspoon meat concentrate (or bouillon cube, crushed)
1¾ cups chicken or beef broth (canned or freshly made)
½ cup California Sauterne, Chablis or other white
    dinner wine
salt and pepper
small toasted French bread slices
grated Parmesan cheese

Peel and thinly slice onions (should be about 2 cups). Cook until soft and golden in butter and oil. Stir in flour and meat concentrate. Add broth, gradually, and bring to a boil. Add wine and salt and pepper, to taste, and simmer for 10 minutes. Place slice of toasted French bread in bottom of soup cup or bowl. Pour in soup and sprinkle generously with cheese.

Modified from the Atlanta Daily World, *October 22, 1963*

Rhubarb and Apple Cobbler Recipe
Serves 6 to 8

4 cups diced rhubarb
2 cups sliced cooking apples
⅔ cup sugar
½ teaspoon salt
⅓ cup unsulfured molasses
2 tablespoons butter or margarine
1 unbaked pastry shell

Heat oven to 450 degrees Fahrenheit. Place rhubarb and apples in 10- by 6- by 2-inch casserole, sprinkling with sugar and salt and dribbling with molasses. Dot with butter. Cover with pastry rolled into a rectangular shape, ⅓ inch thick. Trim, seal and flute edge. Cut a design or gash in pastry to allow steam to escape. Bake 10 minutes; reduce heat to 350 degrees, and bake 30 minutes more, or until crust is brown and fruit is tender.

Modified from the Atlanta Daily World, *April 11, 1952*

With election day not far away, Bobby Kennedy heard that MLK was in jail and behind the scenes called Georgia officials to negotiate a settlement to the conflict. Political pressure, along with the loss of income and negative publicity, influenced Atlanta business owners and Atlanta mayor William Hartsfield to the negotiation table with COAHR leaders. In exchange for the release of Martin Luther King and twenty-three other demonstrators in city jails, leaders of the movement agreed to suspend their demonstrations for thirty days; the mayor wanted the suspension to last sixty or ninety days. Negotiations between demonstrators and state officials continued over the release of thirty-nine demonstrators held for trial on state charges in the county jail. Kennedy's intervention resulted in a political realignment in which large numbers of African Americans supported his brother John Kennedy over Nixon in the November general election.[210]

Demonstrations and failed negotiations would continue for another year. Members of the city's black political establishment met privately with white business leaders and negotiated a settlement in which area lunch counters would be desegregated after the court-ordered integration of city schools the following fall. Although they protested the decision on campus, student leaders finally agreed to the settlement, and Atlanta officials and business owners desegregated lunch counters in the city in September 1961. "We did more than just integrate the lunch counters," said Lonnie King. "We filed a lawsuit—a successful lawsuit—to integrate all the parks/recreation places. We also filed a lawsuit to integrate all the courthouses around here. Now that's not well-known, but we filed the lawsuit, won in federal court, and got all these things."[211] In June

WHERE PEOPLE WENT TO EAT, MEET, REST, PLAN AND STRATEGIZE

1962, members of COAHR such as Ruby Doris and Frank Holloway became members of SNCC's executive committee. Frank Smith, the newly elected chairman of COAHR in 1962, would go on to work for SNCC in Mississippi.[212]

JACKSON, MISSISSIPPI, 1963–1964: THE BIG APPLE INN

The city of Jackson, the state capital of Mississippi, had a vibrant population of black college students, professors and other black professionals in the 1960s. In fact, the students from Jackson State University worked closely with other members of the city's black community in creating a strong civil rights movement.

Hot Business in Hot Tamales

One little-known foodways tradition in the Mississippi Delta are the African American entrepreneurs who sell tamales for a living. One businessman started his successful enterprise on just that food. Juan "Big John" Mora immigrated to Jackson, Mississippi, from Mexico City. He started selling hot tamales out of a cart on Farish Street, the only black-owned and operated business district, where blacks could go to have a good time before the end of segregation. African Americans in Jackson referred to Farish Street, located close to the city's train depot, as Little Harlem because so many black people walked the streets and did their shopping and entertaining there.[213]

After marrying an African American woman, Big John later purchased an old grocery store on Farish Street for $100 in 1939. With his son, Harold, he renovated the store, naming it the Big Apple Inn Restaurant after a popular dance that he loved.[214]

TAMALE PIE

1 can tomatoes
1 can corn
1½ cups yellow cornmeal
1 cup milk
½ pound diced salt pork
2 tablespoons olive oil
1 large onion, minced
1 bell pepper, minced
1 large garlic clove, minced
1 chicken, cooked, deboned and cut into large pieces
1 cup small black olives
2 tablespoons chili powder
salt, to taste
3 eggs

Put tomatoes and corn in a double boiler and cook for 15 minutes. Moisten cornmeal with milk and stir into corn and tomatoes. Cook another 15 minutes. While this is cooking, fry salt pork in olive oil. Remove pork and fry onion, bell pepper and garlic until light brown. Add this, with chicken meat and olives, to mixture. Add chili powder and salt. Beat 3 eggs and fold into mixture. Pour into buttered dish and bake in a moderate oven for 30 minutes.

Modified from the Pittsburgh Courier, *October 18, 1941*

An Eating and Meeting Place for Activists

Like Dooky Chase's Restaurant in New Orleans and Paschal's Restaurant in Atlanta, the Big Apple Inn in Jackson became an important meeting place for civil rights activists, thus helping to literally feed the revolution. Regulars—including civil rights leaders Medger Evers, Fannie Lou Hammer and others affiliated with the NAACP in Mississippi—made their way to Big John's to buy hot sandwiches and tamales made from scratch.[215]

WHERE PEOPLE WENT TO EAT, MEET, REST, PLAN AND STRATEGIZE

Medger Evers was a prominent figure at the Big Apple Inn. After fighting in France and earning the rank of sergeant during World War II, he returned to his home state of Mississippi, earned a college degree, entered the workforce and became a civil rights activist. He became Mississippi's first NAACP field secretary and set up his office over the Big Apple. Because he did not have adequate office space to hold meetings, where he would discuss civil rights organizing and protest strategies, he would often hold them downstairs in the restaurant. When customers came in to buy sandwiches and saw so many people meeting in the restaurant, they inquired as to what was going on. Customers liked what they heard and joined the movement. "In fact, they would be lined up at the [restaurant's] door just to hear Medger's strategy," says Big John's grandson, Gene Lee Sr.[216]

The Big Apple had two signature sandwiches—pig ear sandwiches and hot smoked sausage sandwiches (called smokes) dressed with slaw and mustard, which cost $1 each. The menu also included bologna sandwiches and tamales.[217]

6

THE SANDWICH BRIGADE

THE MARCH ON WASHINGTON FOR JOBS AND FREEDOM

The March on Washington for Jobs and Freedom deputy director Bayard Rustin read to all those assembled in front of the Lincoln Monument on August 28, 1963:

> *The first demand is that we have effective civil rights legislation, no compromise, no filibuster, and that it include public accommodations, decent housing, integrated education, Fair Employment Practices Committee (FEPC) and the right to vote. Number two…we demand the withholding of federal funds from all programs in which discrimination exists. [Third,] we demand that segregation be ended in every school district in the year 1963. [Four,] we demand the enforcement of the 14th Amendment, the reducing of congressional representation of states where citizens are disenfranchised. [Five,] we demand an Executive Order banning discrimination in all housing supported by federal funds. [Six,] we demand that every person in this nation, black or white, be given training and work with dignity to defeat unemployment and automation. [Seven,] we demand that there be an increase in the national minimum wage so that men may live in dignity. [Eight,] we finally demand that all of the rights that are given to any citizen be given to black men and men of every minority group including a strong FEPC.*[218]

In 1963, the country was in a slow, painful recovery from a recession that had begun in 1959. Jobs in manufacturing were shifting to automation, further decreasing the opportunities for employment. Industries that had produced some economic advancement for blacks in the past were slowly becoming nonexistent. Additionally, blacks were barred from advancement in skilled trades due to the discriminatory practices of apprentice systems.[219] The unemployment rate was 5.5 percent, 1.5 million blacks were unemployed and, although blacks made up 11 percent of the workforce, 22 percent were jobless.[220]

Added to the unemployment issue, blacks were protesting against Jim Crow segregation across the South.[221] President Kennedy had been working on a civil rights bill but knew that the legislation would be a tough sell in Congress. He addressed the country, saying, "If an American, because his skin is dark, cannot eat lunch in a restaurant open to the public, if he cannot send his children to the best public schools available, if he cannot vote for the public officials who represent him…then who among us would be content to have the color of his skin changed? Who among us would then be content with counsels of patience and delay?" Kennedy also introduced legislation that would give all Americans "the right to be served in…public restaurants…and similar establishments."[222]

Initially, the president and his brother Bobby, head of the Justice Department, did not support the March on Washington, but the organizers of the march understood the pressure a successful protest in the nation's capital would place on elected politicians and thought it necessary to move forward. March organizers believed that the presence of celebrities would force the Kennedys and others to support it. Singer and social activist Harry Belafonte took up the task of recruiting celebrities, including conservative actor Charlton Heston, to attend. After Belafonte secured the support of celebrities, the Kennedys "cautiously" backed the march, "reassured and impressed by the star power. Instead of some gathering of scruffy activists, this march was starting to sound almost glamorous," said Belafonte.[223]

In contrast, FBI director J. Edgar Hoover covertly did everything within his power to persuade celebrities not to support or attend the march. Hoover "had his agents call each of the actors and entertainers I'd lined up," said Belafonte, "warning them the march might be violent, urging them not to attend. When the march turned out to be peaceful and joyous, the stars would seem to have done a modest thing by showing up. But ignoring those dire FBI warnings, in the days before the march, took some courage."[224]

This section focuses on the role of food in this historic public demonstration and what the organizers, volunteers, citizens and state officials ate on that hot day in late August in the nation's capital. From the beginning, organizers understood that the march's success would in part depend on providing a sufficient supply of food and water for all those attending the event. On the day of the event, concerns grew among the organizers that the people in attendance did not have sufficient food and water supplies. They expected 100,000; in the end, more than 250,000 people marched to the steps of the Lincoln Memorial.[225]

THE "BIG SIX" AND CHURCHES

A. Philip Randolph, the vice-president of the AFL-CIO, put his substantial political capital and organizing skills toward the March on Washington. During the Depression, he threatened a similar march on Washington that forced FDR to end discriminatory practices in the defense industry. He also organized to desegregate the military under President Harry S Truman.

Bayard Rustin (left) and Cleveland Robinson. *Courtesy of Library of Congress.*

He knew the power of peaceful civil disobedience and was a meticulous organizer.[226] Throughout his long career, Randolph put a premium on unity as a way to advance the labor movement's objectives. To that end, he reached out to civil rights leaders, ministers, bureaucrats and elected officials and asked for their help in organizing the march. Labor organizer Cleveland Robinson served as chairman of the March on Washington.[227]

Randolph's civil rights experiences made him beloved among labor leaders and activists. He had stood up to state officials and employers so often that organizers mobilized their grass-roots networks to march on Washington when he asked for support. Randolph was acutely aware that by 1963, the civil rights movement had followers who would turn out in large numbers to protest injustices wherever veteran movement leaders needed them.[228] Randolph called on Rustin, likely the most experienced at planning and executing nonviolent protests, to assist with the initial planning, and Rustin became the chief organizer.

Other civil rights leaders who joined the organizing committee included Roy Wilkins, executive director of the NAACP; Whitney Young Jr., chairman of the Urban League; James Farmer, director of CORE; and John Lewis, chairman of SNCC. They, along with MLK, were referred to as the "Big Six."[229] This diverse group of leaders

Top: Cleveland Robinson at the National Headquarters of the March on Washington in Harlem. *Courtesy of Library of Congress.*

Right: Bayard Rustin at a news briefing in Washington, D.C., in August 1963. *Courtesy of Library of Congress.*

The Big Six civil rights leaders at press conference. *Courtesy of Library of Congress.*

The Big Six and John F. Kennedy in the Oval Office at the White House. *Courtesy of Library of Congress.*

galvanized support within their organizations across the country for the march.

There were four church organizations whose leaders were part of the original planning committee. The National Council of Churches of Christ, the United Presbyterian Church, the American Jewish Congress and the National Catholic Conference were collectively involved in the success of the planning. Organizers sent letters to every church in the nation soliciting support. Ministers, priests and rabbis were urged to speak from the pulpit about the importance of protesting against segregation and involvement in the march. Church congregations responded by sending donations and assisting with food and supplies.[230] Churches provided food to marchers on their way to the march and sent lunches to the marchers in Washington. They also provided space for organizers to gather, usually over meals.

PREPARING MARCHERS

The organizers knew that "a man who is hungry or thirsty or doesn't know where he is going to spend the night may forget why he came to Washington in the first place, i.e., to demonstrate for jobs and freedom."[231] This understanding was a guiding force that led to meticulous planning for the basic needs of the marchers. With the support of labor unions and churches, marchers traveling to Washington from other states were well cared for.

Rustin and Robinson, the chairmen of the Administrative Committee, had eight weeks to plan and organize the march. From their $175,000 operating budget, which was raised from charities and churches, they created a detailed handbook for communicating logistic information. *The March on Washington Organizing Manual* was distributed by the organizing committee leadership to major religious, fraternal, labor and civil rights groups in all of the cities from where marchers were expected. It is unclear how many were printed and how funds for printing them were raised. The manual included specific guidance for food. Organizers recommended that marchers pack two lunches, one for the morning and one for the afternoon. They advised avoiding perishable items like mayonnaise and salads. The suggested items were simple: peanut butter and jelly sandwiches, an apple or other fruit, a brownie or plain cake and a soft drink. It was also advised during the march to "be kind to your stomach—don't eat or drink the wrong foods in the wrong quantities."[232]

Homemade pound cake was common comfort food among southerners and would have likely been part of a marcher's lunch. In the South, particularly in churches, serious competition existed for the title of best baker. Organization and leisure events gave people a chance to show off their baking hands, and it was common for every baker to bring out their prize culinary art to the delight of some and criticism of others. Cookbook author Joyce White remembered these competitions in her Alabama hometown. She observed that the womenfolk "would vie to outdo one another" with their "chocolate cake, pound cake" and other baked goods.[233]

Historically, southerners often served cake, especially pound cakes, for dessert. When World War I started in Europe in 1914, thousands of southerners migrated to the North and Midwest. Many migrants traveled by rail and steamboat, as employers, desperate for laborers, provided free passage. Blacks, accustomed to confronting racist policies while traveling, acquired the habit of packing food for travel on trains and steamboats in empty shoe boxes. They were often stuffed with cold sandwiches, fried chicken, slices of buttered bread, hard-boiled eggs, a little paper of salt and pepper, fruit and a slice of pound cake. When they migrated north to places like Philadelphia, Pittsburgh and New York, southerners carried their culinary traditions, including cake recipes, with them. Nonwhite and non-Protestant travelers would have had to negotiate Jim Crow laws and policies at rest stops and eateries en route to the march.

Organizers urged marchers to prepare wisely to sustain themselves for at least twelve hours. Although the program was scheduled to run two or three hours, most expected the marchers' experience from arrival to departure to last longer. Poppy Cannon White wrote regularly for *Ladies' Home Journal* and *House Beautiful*. She was also the wife of Walter Francis White, a leading figure in the NAACP. She offered her own candid advice on "food for marching" in her column, "Poppy's Notes," which appeared in the *New York Amsterdam News* weeks before the march. White cautioned participants that buying food en route to the march would be expensive. She urged marchers to consider foods that would sustain and comfort them on what promised to be a long, hot summer day. She warned that the food should be "light in weight, non-bulky, and non-squashable or drippy."[234]

White's recommendations included hard-cooked eggs, hard salami, firm cheeses and crusty breads or rolls. She also preferred raw vegetables like carrots, radishes and celery hearts to others that might wilt in the heat. One of her readers suggested she assemble the proper items in what she could call a "Freedom Feedbag," sell it and donate the profits to the cause. While a novel idea, there is no evidence that White pursued the proposal.[235]

BOX LUNCHES AND THE SANDWICH BRIGADE

Deputy Director of the March Committee Rustin said that his committee had budgeted $75,000 for the entire event and "allocated $15,000 of its budget for bringing the poor and jobless from the South to the march."[236]

Rustin and Randolph enlisted the help of a coalition of organizations throughout the country to ensure that anyone who came unprepared would have a food resource available to them. Organizers called on groups and an army of volunteers to prepare food for those in need on the day of the march. The National Council of Churches called on workers to help prepare the eighty thousand box lunches that were on hand for the march.[237]

Literary great James Weldon Johnson grew up in Jacksonville, Florida, and attended Atlanta University in Atlanta, Georgia, at the turn of the century. He recalled, "In those days, no one would think of boarding a train without a [box] lunch, not even for a trip of two or three hours; and no lunch was a real lunch that did not consist of fried chicken, slices of buttered bread, hard-boiled

A food service crew prepares box lunches for the March on Washington. *Courtesy of the National Archives.*

Volunteer workers prepare box lunches at Riverside Church for the March on Washington. *Courtesy of Library of Congress.*

eggs, a little paper of salt and pepper, an orange or two, and a piece of cake."[238] Similarly, thousands of African Americans who traveled to Washington, D.C., for the March on Washington did so with box lunches on trains and buses.

Riverside Church in Harlem, New York, was at the center of organizing efforts due to its location near the organizing committee headquarters, also in Harlem. Rustin referred to this group as the "sandwich brigade."[239] Two days before the march, volunteers worked in three-hour shifts at the church. They worked for two days and two nights preparing the lunches.[240] One hundred volunteers started at 6:00 a.m. making the box lunches sold at the march. They were relieved by one hundred more at the end of their shift. The groups of volunteers were "multi-denominational and interfaith as well as interracial."[241] They spent hours assembling the lunches that included "$40,000 worth of cheese, bread, and apples that had been donated by charities and purchased with operating funds."[242]

Careful consideration went into the box lunch. Reverend Walter Fauntroy, who was in charge of the Washington office of the march, insisted that the lunches be kept to a minimum. Organizers told marchers as well as volunteers who donated food to only include nonperishable food items in their lunches, which was something that food writer Poppy Cannon White had recommended in her column. Mayonnaise was avoided and, perhaps for economic reasons, meat was not included on the sandwiches that were prepared and distributed from the Harlem headquarters. The lunches consisted of an American cheese sandwich, a packet of mustard, an apple, and a slice of marble or pound cake. Other types of fruit and hard candy were also considered but omitted, but it's unclear why. The box lunches sold for fifty cents.[243]

Organizers enlisted the help of Blaikie, Miller and Hines Inc., a New York City catering company, to assist with management of the production process. Details about the process and how things were assembled are not available in the historical record. One Catholic priest who brought some of his parishioners described the operation as the "largest split-second food packing operation ever undertaken in the city."[244] Once the lunches were prepared, the Church World Service, the relief division of the World Council of Churches, transported the donated lunches in a refrigerated truck.

Traveling from Near and Far

Marchers came to Washington by foot, car, bus, train and plane. They came from all across the country. Carrying duffel bags, knapsacks and shopping bags, they lined up to board buses while businesses and charities prepared to support the travelers.[245] Carol Ardman traveled by bus from New York City to Washington, D.C. She recalled, "Every seat was taken, and there were many buses, all going in a caravan." En route to the march, the caravan stopped at a rest stop with a Howard Johnson's restaurant. She remembered people on the bus getting off and "swarming" the vending machines for candy bars and quickly emptying them all. "I hadn't brought any food with me and I was alone, but I believe my seat-mate shared her peanut butter sandwich with me." Ardman added, "I didn't eat much that day, so I was hungry."[246]

Nancy Schimmel belonged to the San Francisco chapter of the organization Women for Peace. She and other members of the group traveled to the march on a CORE-sponsored bus all the way from San Francisco, California. "We ate in bus station cafés on the way there and

CORE members from Fort Hamilton Parkway in Brooklyn start on their trek for the March on Washington. *Courtesy of Library of Congress.*

Marchers arrive by bus. One man carries a lunchbox. *Courtesy of Library of Congress.*

Above: Marchers arrive at Union Station. *Courtesy of Library of Congress.*

Right: Harry Belafonte and other Hollywood actors arrive by plane. *Courtesy of Library of Congress.*

back," she remembered. "The bus driver [persuaded] us to let him take us to the Amana Colony restaurant in Iowa instead of the bus station (he was so right!)." The bus would go on to stop at a bus stop with a Howard Johnson's near Washington, D.C., where she saw "some SNCC kids in overalls," which made her realize "this was really happening." The bus arrived the day before the march. That night, she and her group attended a dinner that the D.C. Women for Peace chapter hosted and spent the night in the area at an unnamed university in dorm rooms. In the morning, they ate breakfast in the school cafeteria and then headed off to the march. She said, "I have no memory of eating lunch....Maybe we didn't, maybe we bought sandwiches at the cafeteria to take with us."[247]

Five thousand members of the Retail, Wholesale and Department Store Union provided lunches and suppers to people traveling to the march. The International Ladies' Garment Workers Union provided eight thousand box lunches to travelers from New York City, Newark, Philadelphia, eastern Pennsylvania, Long Island, Baltimore and other points in the Northeast.[248]

In the weeks leading up to the march, Benton Caldon, the manager of the Howard Johnson's rest stop in Cranbury, New Jersey, which is fifty-three miles south of New York, was planning for the increase in highway traffic. He knew the fourteen rest stops along the route from New Jersey to Washington, D.C., would be busy and geared up to accommodate the increased number of buses and cars traveling to the march. The company expanded parking areas, extended hours of operation and increased its supply of refreshments. The rest stop refreshment inventory increased to include 6,000 half-pint containers of soft drinks, 2,400 half pints of milk, 2,400 ham sandwiches, twelve thousand frankfurters and 5,400 chicken halves.[249]

Churches in Washington, D.C., that marchers passed along the route to the Lincoln Memorial included St. Stephens and the Incarnation Episcopal Church at Sixteenth and Newton Streets Northwest, St. John's Episcopal Church at Sixteenth and H Streets Northwest and St. Patrick's Catholic Church at Tenth and Chevy Chase Circle. When local and out-of-state marchers stopped at any of these churches, they could get a hot breakfast of ham and eggs or a hot supper with fried chicken. It's unclear if these were free or if everyone paid for their meal. Historically, most African American churches did not charge for the food at their events. Hospitality ministries organized, cooked and served refreshments at church events.[250]

Fried chicken was the meat most often served in black churches at the time. It was referred to by many as the "gospel bird" and is a common fixture of church traditions. Throughout history, chicken had a permanent place on the tables and in the boxed lunches and picnic baskets of southerners and blacks in the North and the South. Before their arrival in North America, West Africans ate poultry on special occasions as part of their religious ceremonies. Travel accounts dating back to before the 1800s show West African women batter-frying chicken. In many ways, fried chicken is an example of an African practice continued when Africans came to North America during the Atlantic slave trade. During the antebellum period, most enslaved Africans only had time to make labor-intensive fried chicken on days their master gave them off, such as Sundays, a few holidays and religious days. Frying became the preferred method of cooking chicken during this period because it was quick and required only a large pot and few utensils. The practice of frying chicken continued into the twentieth century.[251]

Despite resistance from some church congregations, there was strong overall support from the religious community for the march. Breaking bread with marchers in a house of worship gave supporters a sense of solidarity with traveling marchers. Throughout the march, participants seemed to embrace the sense of solidarity across communities. They did this in a variety of settings where food was shared. The time of fellowship

Southern Christian Leadership Conference (SCLC) for the Savannah Freedom Now Movement. *Courtesy of Library of Congress.*

Marchers with a District 65 ALF-CIO sign. *Courtesy of Library of Congress.*

Marchers with a National Council of Negro Women sign. *Courtesy of Library of Congress.*

A. Philip Randolph and other civil rights leaders on their way to Congress. *Courtesy of Library of Congress.*

Demonstrators march in the street. *Courtesy of Library of Congress.*

likely reinforced the marchers' connection to a common set of ethics and values that are rooted in religious teachings of varying faiths.[252] The march's ecumenical and multiethnic dimension along with the protesters adherence to nonviolence gave it increased credibility among detractors who predicted gloom, doom and violence.

"LIKE A CHURCH PICNIC"

On the day of the march, police officials described the beginning hours as a "very slow and steady march, almost like a church picnic." One reporter observed, "They seem quite leisurely....Most of them are just walking. Some are eating their boxed lunches as they go along. This group right here now is singing. They're carrying signs saying, 'We demand an end to bias now.' Another one says, 'No U.S. dough to help Jim Crow grow.'"[253]

The weather that day was not unbearable, which could be the case on a typical Washington, D.C. August day. According to a National Weather Service spokesman, the high was eighty-three and the low sixty-three, with no precipitation. Dew points were comfortably low, staying in the fifties.[254]

Other marchers like Mr. and Mrs. Robert Hall of Richmond, Virginia, rested their weary feet and enjoyed an unnamed snack near the wading pool. At the Reflecting Pool, multiethnic attenders from around the county took out their picnic baskets and ate. People sat together, ate and waited for the start of the two-hour-long program. Some sat on picnic blankets as they shared their cold drinks or cake with other marchers. Others sat on the edge of the wading pool with their feet submerged for a cool bit of relief. All waited with eager anticipation for the coming events. About noon, marchers started to make their way closer to the Lincoln Memorial, the site of the speakers' podium for the demonstration.[255] Harry Belafonte started rounding up the contingent of celebrities he had recruited for the event back at their hotels to load a bus headed for the Lincoln Monument. They departed the bus at the far end of the Reflecting Pool. "Tens of thousands of people had already made the walk here from the Washington Monument," Belafonte remembered. "Many were cooling their feet in the Reflecting Pool."[256]

Police officials announced that starting the day before and ending the day after, officers had overtime requirements, some as long as eighteen-hour shifts. Also, government officials had to prepare "7,000 box lunches and dinners" to feed on-duty officers at a cost of over $5,000. In an

An aerial view of marchers, from the Lincoln Monument to the Washington Monument.
Courtesy of Library of Congress.

unprecedented move, the District of Columbia commissioners banned the sale of all alcoholic beverages, including beer and wine. The ban also applied to bars, restaurants and liquor stores in the area.[257] Whether this decision was racially motivated or intended as an added measure to help with crowd control is unknown. We do know that FBI director Hoover, who was not an advocate of the march, predicted that the event would be violent and that activists and communists would destroy the city on the day of the march.[258] Other federal officials seemed to have agreed with Hoover. "Less than half a mile away [from the Lincoln Memorial], discreetly hidden, were tanks and other combat vehicles, and troops armed to the teeth," recalled Belafonte. "But with not a hint of violence emanating from the crowd, the military might would remain where it was. Most in the crowd would have no idea it was there."[259]

Meanwhile, a report from the march around noon indicated that the numbers of people who had come without food and water had started complaining about needing them. They may have been city residents, federal and city employees and/or tourists who came to see the demonstration without planning on staying for more than four hours. Others came with food and water but not enough for what turned out to be a more than ten-hour event. When asked around 1:00 p.m. what comments he was hearing from the marchers, one reporter said, "Most people are hungry and thirsty and most people also want to move into the areas restricted for the fortunate like those of us of the press."[260]

There was, however, food for sale at the march. Government Services Incorporated (GSI), a private company with a franchise permitted to sell food in areas supervised by the National Park Service, stored the cheese sandwich lunches that were made at the Harlem headquarters. The GSI sold the lunches in refreshment stands set up throughout the park grounds. In addition, hot dogs and soft drinks were also sold by GSI at six refreshment stands. Ice cream vendors were allowed to sell cold snacks throughout the grounds that day as well.[261]

VIP PROVISIONS AND SPACE

Organizers of the event provided VIPs like Belafonte and other celebrities with an uncrowded, restricted area behind the Lincoln Memorial that contained an abundance of food and beverages. We "had our own little

Above: Charlton Heston and Harry Belafonte arrive. *Courtesy of Library of Congress.*

Right: Sammy Davis Jr., waving to people. *Courtesy of Library of Congress.*

holding pen, with tables of drinks and sandwiches," Belafonte recalled. "For a while, we just mingled. The union leaders were there, too, and writers—everyone whose presence I'd thought would help elevate the occasion."[262]

In an interview given within the VIP space, Belafonte said, "This is the first time in the history of a major civil rights gathering" that so many artists have demonstrated their solidarity with the civil rights movement. A partial list of noted artists in attendance at the march includes writer James Baldwin; singers Mahalia Jackson, Bob Dylan, Joan Baez and Odessa; comedian and activist Dick Gregory; and actor, actresses and entertainers Marlon Brando, James Garner, Sammy Davis Jr., Joanne Woodward, Susan Strasberg, Burt Lancaster, Robert Ryan, Sidney Poitier, Diahann Carroll, Gregory Peck, Anthony Quinn, Paul Newman, Charlton Heston, Irwin Shaw, Lena Horne, Ruby Dee and Josephine Baker. Baker and Baldwin had traveled to D.C. from their homes in Paris. Burt Lancaster also brought a list of 1,500 entertainers from Paris who could not attend the march but stood in solidarity with those who could.[263]

There was a noticeable difference between the treatment of the masses of people who attended the march and that of those with celebrity status, the entertainers, labor leaders and intellectuals. The food and water planning for the event can best be described as insufficient. However, about two and a

A crowd of people at the Lincoln Memorial. *Courtesy of Library of Congress.*

THE SANDWICH BRIGADE

A woman with a camera stands in front of the crowd. *Courtesy of Library of Congress.*

Demonstrators take a break to eat sandwiches. *Courtesy of Library of Congress.*

half times more people attended the event than the organizers had expected. The organizers did a fairly good job of providing free and inexpensive box lunches and makeshift water fountains on a limited budget and with limited time to prepare. Dehydration proved the biggest problem, which in retrospect is understandable considering that the march occurred before the invention of inexpensive bottled water and other containers event organizers can use today.

FROM MUSLIM SOUP TO THE FAMOUS BEAN PIE

FOOD BUSINESSES AND THE PURSUIT OF ECONOMIC EMPOWERMENT

The bulk of the negroes were either on welfare or WPA or they starved. [W]e were much better off than most of the town negroes. The reason was we raised much of our own food out there in the country where we were. Not only did we have our big garden, but we raised chickens....I loved [having my own garden plot] and took care of it well. I loved especially to grow peas. I was proud when we had them on our table. I would pull out the grass in my garden by hand when the first little blades came up....And sometimes when I had everything straight and clean for my things to grow, I would lay down on my back between two rows and I would gaze up in the blue sky at the clouds moving and think all kinds of things.[264]

The above passage shows a side of Malcolm X most people don't know. Malcolm loved gardening and later become the spokesman of the Nation of Islam (or the "Nation" hereafter), an organization that championed black economic independence and operated farms toward that end. In 1995, Louis Farrakhan, who had once been one of Malcolm's protégés, held the position of leader of the Nation. Farrakhan called for the Million Man March on Washington, which they did. This chapter takes a historic farm-to-table culinary look at the Nation.

African Americans have an entrepreneurial legacy of growing produce and cooking and selling food that dates back to before their arrival in the Americas. They sold food in local and long-distance African markets and had established

Malcolm X, 1964. *Courtesy of Library of Congress.*

farmers' markets long before the term became in vogue in the twentieth century. After their arrival in North America, enterprising free and enslaved food vendors sold enough to, over time, save ample money to open brick-and-mortar grocery stores, restaurants, taverns and boardinghouses. Selling food created a chance to go into business for oneself and of possibly purchasing the freedom of loved ones who were still enslaved. For the farmer, street vendor or restaurant owner, food grown and/or cooked inexpensively and sold at a profit could provide an avenue to increased economic independence.

ELIJAH MUHAMMAD AND THE NATION OF ISLAM

Born Elijah Robert Poole in Sandersville, Georgia, in 1897, Elijah Muhammad built and led the Nation of Islam in the United States from 1934 until his death in 1975. During the Great Depression, Muhammad migrated to Detroit, where he met Wallace Fard Muhammad, who became his religious mentor in his study of a distinctively U.S. Black Nationalist interpretation of Islam. After the departure of Fard Muhammad, Elijah Muhammad would go on to start the Nation of Islam around 1940 in Detroit and thereafter moved its headquarters to Chicago.[265] In Chicago, Muhammad built a black Muslim empire that reached across the United States, with its greatest recruiting successes among poor blacks and Black Nationalists, such as black Hebrews and members of the UNIA in Chicago, Detroit, Boston, Pittsburgh, Newark, Los Angeles and New York.[266] In many ways built on the economic development model of the UNIA, by 1960,

Elijah Muhammad addresses his followers, 1964. *Courtesy of Library of Congress.*

Muhammad Ali attending a Nation of Islam Meeting, 1964. *Courtesy of Library of Congress.*

the Nation of Islam had smaller groups of followers in southern cities like Washington, D.C., and Atlanta.

Muhammad sent Malcolm X, perhaps the Nation's best evangelist in the 1950s, to organize new temples. In New York, Malcolm evangelized in Harlem near hot spots known for Black Nationalist revolutionary activity. He also recruited around storefront churches noted for good preaching where southern migrants attended. The Nation also fished among the black working class and underclass. Convicts and ex-convicts were another target group for Malcolm X and other Nation of Islam evangelists.[267]

Young, poor African Americans found the organization's message appealing. Eighty percent of its ministers and those who attended its temple tended to be under age thirty-five. An increase in media coverage of the Nation of Islam in mainstream outlets during the 1960s worked to increase its membership roll. By 1960, the Nation had an estimated membership of fifty to seventy thousand people with about ten thousand dedicated members who changed their last name to X, denouncing their former slave masters' names.[268] Converts removed pork and alcohol

FROM MUSLIM SOUP TO THE FAMOUS BEAN PIE

Malcolm X greets Martin Luther King before a press conference, 1964. *Courtesy of Library of Congress.*

The Nation of Islam Office in Harlem. *Courtesy of Library of Congress.*

from their diets and ate one meal a day. They abstained from gambling, smoking, drinking, overeating and buying on credit. As a result, most rank-and-file members enjoyed a healthy standard of living and still had enough money left to support the organization.[269]

THE NATION'S ECONOMIC BLUEPRINT

Elijah Muhammad and his ministers taught members of the organization to give one-third of their income to their mosque each year. In addition, local mosques collected contributions for various local and national initiatives that Muhammad launched out of his Chicago headquarters. The nation "advocate[s] a complete economic withdrawal from the white community," said sociologist C. Eric Lincoln.[270] To accomplish that goal, they set about developing businesses. The Nation started food businesses with the goal of reducing their dependence on white-controlled businesses, minimizing contact with whites and increasing "jobs and capital for black workers and entrepreneurs," explained Lincoln.[271] Muhammad developed an "Economic Blueprint," published "in some element of the black press and serv[ing] as the basic text for" his public sermons given in rented halls across the country used to encourage the faithful and to recruit new members.[272] The essentials of the economic blueprint called for recognizing the necessity of unity, pooling one's resources, learning from white business owners and buying black whenever possible. Ministers taught that Muslims must learn to provide for their own using skills and methods gleaned from whites. Muhammad taught his followers that many of the problems that plagued African Americans had been economic.[273]

In the 1960s, Muhammad championed "economic unity among black people…as one step toward building economic independence" for black people, as he said in the organization-owned and operated newspaper *Muhammad Speaks*. The paper would go on to become one of the organization's most important methods for disseminating its views to its members and nonmembers, particularly those living in poor black urban neighborhoods.[274] He spent the lion's share of his time focused on developing the Nation's economic blueprint, which he designed in part from a historical memory of Garvey's UNIA and NFC of the 1920s. In contrast to the UNIA's "back to Africa" emphasis, the Nation focused on building its own black state in the United States. "We're going to have our own all-black state," Malcolm

X told a newspaper reporter in 1960—an independent entity with its own government, diplomatic corps, treasury and departments of commerce and agriculture. The Nation sought a black country within the United States about the size of five states within the Union as reparations for slavery.[275]

About 1964, Elijah Muhammad predicted the economic collapse of the United States. He moved to expand the organization's landholdings in the Southwest as a way of providing for the economic needs of black Americans. Members John Muhammad and Malcolm Shah staked a claim on land in Fort Worth, Texas. Next, the two began chopping down twenty-three trees in a park before they attracted the attention of park employees, who had assumed they had also been park employees. The sighting of a Muslim star and crescent moon emblem aroused suspicion, leading to their arrest.[276]

Elijah Muhammad sought land for the establishment of farms and related food-processing facilities. The farms and the processing plants would provide products for retail food businesses near mosques. Muhammad said, "We are twenty-two million or more people depending on the white American citizens to produce food, clothes, shelter, transportation, employment, and our educational training. If you say we cannot unite, you are wrong. We can unite!"[277] Like Garvey, Muhammad championed African Americans patronizing black-owned businesses. Both leaders started and assisted others in the establishment of businesses that they expected the members of their organization to support.[278]

Muhammad had been sharing his vision for starting food businesses in black communities in the pages of *Muhammad Speaks*, which members of the organization sold in urban centers across the United States. In one of his messages, he insisted that "the black man in America must have some of this earth he can call his own, must reap the economic harvest from his own community, or control the enterprises which he patronizes. The black man must do what only he alone can do for himself!" He went on to say, "The day of white domination nears an end and that end will come sooner when black community and business leaders, tradesmen, educators, laborers unite behind Muhammad to pool their resources."[279]

During the civil rights movement of the 1950s and 1960s, the Nation served as an alternative to the NAACP, CORE, SNCC and other groups engaged in a nonviolent strategy to advance the interest of black people. Picketing against businesses that discriminated against black customers represented the Nation's most visible sign of civil rights protest. Later, the Nation opposed armed revolution as a strategy toward black uplift during the black power movement of the late 1960s and thereafter. In 1968,

Above: Elijah Muhammad addresses an assembly of the Nation of Islam in 1964. *Courtesy of Library of Congress.*

Left: An image of Elijah Muhammad with a marketing poster of Economic Blue Print. *Courtesy of Magnum Photo.*

Muhammad advocated self-help programs that helped black communities instead of throwing bricks or Molotov cocktails. In the pages of the organization's periodical, he wrote, "The black man must be given an equal chance to do something for himself and for his own."[280]

Between about 1965 and 1966, the Nation obtained and operated a combination of ten thousand acres of farmland in Michigan, Alabama and Georgia dedicated to cultivating food crops, cows, chickens and sheep. In addition, it operated its own slaughterhouse and shipped its own goods to market. A representative of the Nation, C. Eric Lincoln, reported in *The Black Muslims in America*:

> *We presently deal with truckloads of produce coming and going from places as far away as California, Texas, Georgia, and Alabama and as near (to the home office in Chicago) as Michigan, Wisconsin, Indiana, etc. We cater not only to our Muslim-owned businesses. The Messenger created* GOOD FOODS CORP., *which serves chain stores and individually owned markets large and small, giving them all the best in produce, meats, eggs, poultry, and fish. We market truckloads of beef every week with one truckload holding 35,000 pounds. We produce and sell 12,000 dozens of eggs a week and we need more. One dairy alone gives us 2,200 gallons of milk per week and we need to increase that. Our apple orchard gave us 25,000 3-lb. bags of apples and this was not sufficient to meet the demand. We handled thirty truckloads of watermelons, each containing approximately 40,000 pounds. We warehouse hundreds of 100-lb. bags of navy beans, which depart each week from the warehouse to be consumed by people in many ways, from Muslim soup to the famous bean pie. We slaughter and sell over 200 lambs a day. We sell thousands of pounds of fish a week in our local fish markets. We transport these food items in our own trucks and on our own plane to markets around the country. If we are not in your area now, we soon will be.[281]*

The Nation also operated bakeries, a large supermarket and restaurants. Its retail food businesses focused on healthier food and better service than what was available to most African Americans at the time. The elegant white tablecloth Shabazz Restaurant in Chicago served as the Nation's first foray into opening a formal dining restaurant. The Nation claimed that its excellent food, aesthetics, comfort and courteous and efficient service served as its trademark. Its menu included "baked chicken, roast beef, and Salisbury steak [and] the finest in salads, vegetables, and desserts."[282] Josephine

A Nation of Islam grocery store. *Courtesy of Magnum Photo.*

Harris of the Mount Olive Missionary Baptist Church in Chicago described her dining experience there as superb. "The cooking was exquisite and the waitresses and entire personnel were courteous, charming, and warm. We found relaxing surroundings and a friendly and charming staff," she said. Harris added, "There can be no better atmosphere in which to enjoy an evening of dining and conversation."[283] In 1968, the Nation opened a large, elegant white tablecloth restaurant called Salaam, also in Chicago.

Muhammad Speaks described the restaurant as "one of the largest and most dazzling" in the world.[284]

In addition to its eateries in Chicago, the Nation operated a cafeteria in Harlem, a café in Atlanta and a grocery store in Washington, D.C.[285] A *Wall Street Journal* reporter provided a bird's-eye view of the Nation's restaurant in Harlem:

> *The Temple Number Seven Restaurant…is located on Lenox Avenue in the heart of Harlem and around the corner from the movement's Mosque.…The restaurant…is spotless. In the front there is a counter with about a dozen seats. To the rear there are ten four-seat tables, each adorned with a vase of wax flowers. The walls are decorated with a large portrait of Elijah Muhammad and a giant color enlargement of a sphinx.*[286]

In contrast to soul food restaurants, the Nation's restaurants served beef and fish meals with brown rice, fresh vegetables, bean soup and bean pies.[287]

BEAN PIE

"Pies are made of odd vegetables like sweet potatoes and squash, carrots and pumpkin, of course. But who ever heard of a bean pie? We discovered it…featured in the restaurant Shabazz run by the followers of Islam [who] adapted the Middle Eastern inspired dish to suite the tastes of Southerners. As prepared by the Muslim ladies of the mosque, the bean pie requires soaking navy beans or pea beans overnight and fairly long cooking."
—Poppy Cannon, food writer, *Chicago Daily Defender*

Serves 6 to 8

1 28-ounce can cooked navy beans
2 cups milk
3 tablespoons butter, melted
½ cup dark brown sugar
½ cup white sugar
3 eggs, well beaten

---

1 teaspoon cinnamon
¼ teaspoon ginger
¼ teaspoon nutmeg
¼ teaspoon black pepper (believe it or not)
2 teaspoons vanilla
2 unbaked 9-inch pastry shells

Pour beans into blender and combine with milk, melted butter, dark brown and white sugar, well beaten eggs, cinnamon, ginger, nutmeg, black pepper and vanilla. Pour into two unbaked pie pastry shells and bake in a moderately hot oven (375 degrees Fahrenheit) for about 30 minutes, or until a silver knife inserted in the center comes out clean. Pies will puff up in the oven but flatten when removed. Like sweet potato and pumpkin pies, which they resemble, these pies are best when served slightly warm. May be topped with whipped or ice cream. They freeze beautifully. Cut into serving pieces before freezing so that you can remove a wedge—or two, or three—as wanted.[288]

Modified from the Chicago Daily Defender, *July 23, 1968*

In the 1960s, Eugene Watts operated a barbershop on Third Street in Mount Vernon, New York. Next to his shop was a restaurant called Philly's Bake and Take, owned by a member of the Nation of Islam. The restaurant "did really, really good" business, said Watts. "I still hear people, and this has been over fifteen years, talk about how they miss that restaurant." The restaurant's cook at one time was a "Sister Lana." She also cooked for the Muslim convert and heavyweight champion Muhammad Ali and "would go down to Harlem to Temple 7 and help them prepare food and then come up here to Mount Vernon." Her specialty, recalled Watts, was bean soup. "That was an important staple for Muslims, the great northern bean. And [Sister Lana] would fix it in such a way that people would be lined up out the door to get a cup of this soup....These were regular [non-Muslim customers]." When people heard that Sister Lana was in town, they quickly made their way over to Third Street.[289]

Afterword

OCCUPY WALL STREET

SEPTEMBER 17, 2011, TO NOVEMBER 15, 2011

On July 13, 2011, *Adbusters*, an anti-consumerism magazine based in Vancouver, British Columbia, Canada, published a blog post calling for "a shift in revolutionary tactics" and urging people to converge on lower Manhattan. The plan was to "set up tents, kitchens, peaceful barricades, and occupy Wall Street for a few months. Once there, we shall incessantly repeat one simple demand in a plurality of voices." What was that demand? A presidential commission to end corporate control over representative government. The same post introduced the hashtag #occupywallstreet. Organizers launched the Occupy Wall Street website on July 26, 2011, and began using Twitter and Facebook to mobilize supporters on September 17, 2011.[290]

Zuccotti Park became the symbolic flagship campus of the movement. By October, organized labor openly supported protesters in the park. Under the slogan "We are the 99%," the Occupy Wall Street movement (OWS) spread to 350 other cities across the country, most of them much smaller than Manhattan. On October 12, protesters withstood New York mayor Michael Bloomberg's threat to evict them from the park, which further strengthened the movement.

The flagship campus, like the smaller movements elsewhere, included a kitchen work group. The "People's Kitchen" at Zuccotti Park received donations from around the world that helped them serve three thousand meals a day for free. Members of the People's Kitchen continually fed the OWS revolution until a police eviction on November 15, 2011, ended the occupation of the park.[291] The *New York Times* food writer Mark Bittman viewed the occupiers as part of a global struggle to fix a broken capitalist system. He called them a diverse revolutionary movement for positive change in solidarity with activists in Argentina, Spain, Tunisia, Egypt and Greece.[292]

This afterword focuses on the OWS movement and looks at its precursors. OWS and its People's Kitchen in Zuccotti Park came from the historical memory and examples of organizers around the world. It had not been a new strategy, and it has proven to be a method for supporting movements for progressive change and ending hunger around the world. In addition to the movements covered in earlier chapters, what movements influenced OWS and its People's Kitchen? What individuals and groups made important food-related contributions? The majority of the answers to these questions are based on interviews I conducted in October 2011 at Zuccotti Park.

PRECURSORS

Several movements that have needed to feed thousands of people on a daily basis have used a consensus decision-making process that some have coined "horizontal democracy" and others have called "circled justice." Whatever the term, it seems to have its origins in Native American institutions. In southern Mexico, the Zapatista movement did this when it launched its armed rebellion in Chiapas, Mexico, in 1994. Similarly, after the economic collapse in Argentina in 2001, activists there organized into working groups to meet basic needs.[293] In each of these movements, people came together to organize ways of supporting one another, including providing basic necessities, such as food and beverages. Depending on their interests, skills and leanings, participants in the movement created popular kitchens, with the kitchen working group deciding how members of that group would acquire and prepare the food and beverages distributed for free to people each day.[294]

In October 2010, a movement in Spain began when 200,000 people marched in Madrid to protest high unemployment, mortgage reforms and the general economic crisis in that country for which elected officials had provided no solutions. The movement culminated with some 10,000 people occupying one of Spain's most visible public spaces—Puerta del Sol, a plaza in Madrid. They came to be known as the *indignados*. The group organized into small committees charged with providing basic necessities, such as food, beverages and bedding. They used smartphones and Twitter to publicize their takeover of the plaza, using the hashtag #acampadasol. Some 20,000 people came to participate in the occupation, which lasted until July 2011. After the end of the occupation, the movement spread across Spain in different manifestations.[295]

The direct actions of a twenty-six-year-old Tunisian fruit vendor named Mohamed Bouazizi ignited what became known as the Jasmine Revolution. On a December morning in 2010, he resisted the attempt of government authorities to confiscate equipment he used to earn a living selling fruit to provide for his immediate and extended family. His resistance and later protest represented years of bottled-up frustration that came from the daily exasperations rank-and-file Tunisians experienced in a society built on bribing officials, injustice and government neglect, as well from the fact that the well-connected had access to opportunities that the majority of citizens could only dream of. His struggle with government representatives and subsequent self-inflicted death as a protest mobilized masses of disenfranchised and frustrated Tunisian citizens to overthrow three brutal dictatorships in North Africa.[296]

This revolution represents an example of the role a food-related business played in starting a social movement. Egyptians took to the streets after the start of the Tunisian revolution. Protesters mobilized to end the police state of President Hosni Mubarak and domestic policies that included cuts in government food subsidies, increased food prices, which contributed to increasing levels of unemployment and underemployment for college graduates.[297]

On October 25, 2011, Asmaa Mahfouz, a Tahrir activist, visited Zuccotti Park and shared with organizers there the importance activists in Egypt had placed on building coalitions with organized labor. She also incited activists in New York to increase their boldness in advancing their demands. For example, when she led a group of protesters down Wall Street, she took the lead in defiantly stepping off the police-established protest route.[298]

In addition to the movements in Europe and North Africa, OWS happened after more recent U.S. movements that had gone underreported in the media. For example, teaching assistants in New York occupied a university building at the New School in December 2009 in their struggle for union representation. Organized labor in Wisconsin occupied the state capitol in February 2011 when Republican Governor Scott Walker sought to roll back workers' rights, such as collective bargaining, healthcare and retirement benefits. And in June 2011, protestors in New York City created a three-week-long "Bloombergville" in protest of the policies of Mayor Michael Bloomberg and what they called the selling of city government to corporate interests, particularly realtors.[299]

ZUCCOTTI PARK

What individuals and groups made important food-related contributions? I first visited Zuccotti Park, the OWS flagship campus, on a cold and windy day in October. The majority of protesters can best be described as similar to those participating in the movements in Spain and North Africa: young, unemployed people from the middle class, educated folks, first-time protesters and a sprinkling of old and young veteran activists.[300]

The kitchen work group established the People's Kitchen in the middle of the park. They established makeshift pantries stacked with boxes of plastic wrap, aluminum foil, paper towels, napkins and plastic utensils. I saw popcorn in large garbage bags and shelves filled with canned Goya beans and tuna fish. Another shelf had vinegar and various unopened bottles of salad dressing. Below that were various herbs and seasonings and salt. Another shelf held a bottle of honey and several containers of peanut butter. I saw plastic bins with loads of bread, mostly multigrain. There were enough Gatorade-type water coolers for a summer youth lacrosse tournament. There were portable coffee and tea containers like those used by catering companies for outdoor events. Bottled water was stacked everywhere. They had prep tables set up with cutting boards, loaves of bread on deck to

People's Kitchen volunteers get ready for the breakfast meal at Zuccotti Park, New York City. *Courtesy of Food Prof Photos.*

Taking inventory of supplies at the People's Kitchen. *Courtesy of Food Prof Photos.*

Pantry full of donated napkins, plates and cleaning necessities. *Courtesy of Food Prof Photos.*

be cut, apples and oranges and a bagel slicer. On their serving tables, I saw rice, almond and soy milk containers from Trader Joe's; apple juice; ketchup bottles; hand sanitizer; Clif MOJO bars; and breakfast bars from Trader Joe's. Another table had all types of sliced bread, a tray full of Smucker's jams of all varieties and a single jar of peanut butter. There were boxes of apples marked "Saratoga, New York" that looked fresh-picked. There were trays filled with peanut butter and jam sandwiches made with all kinds of delicious-looking, multigrain, artisanal breads. Behind another serving table, I saw a prep area where someone had started cutting carrots for a salad. Next to the cutting board was a single tomato, a large bag of celery and a large plastic box full of salad greens. Members of the People's Kitchen could be easily identified because they wore the plastic gloves one sees in the restaurant industry. There was a donation bucket clearly marked on one of the tables. It all looked like a tailgate at a fall football game at a U.S. bohemian college campus.

I was surprised to hear a British accent among the members of the People's Kitchen staff. I asked the speaker, Bob, where he was from.

"Originally from England," he answered. "I have been in the United States for forty years."

Stacked bottled waters and coolers at People's Kitchen. *Courtesy of Food Prof Photos.*

Above: Donated fruit at People's Kitchen *Courtesy of Food Prof Photos.*

Right: Donated Trader Joe's bars and granola bars at People's Kitchen. *Courtesy of Food Prof Photos.*

"And how long have you been down at Occupy Wall Street?"

"I just got here," he said.

"So, what do you think? You've seen other movements like this?"

"Absolutely," he said.[301]

As a nineteen-year-old student attending the University of London, Bob had joined the Campaign for Nuclear Disarmament (CND) that mobilized for the demilitarization of the United Kingdom nuclear weapons and advancing the proliferation of non-nuclear peace agreements around the world. Since 1957, when British activist Bertrand Russell and others organized the CND, it has been at the forefront of the UK peace movement.[302]

Bob joined the anti-nuclear movement when it came to the United States. He recalls serving as a member of the kitchen work group during what *Time* magazine called the "Siege at Seabrook." During the early 1970s, activists opposed to nuclear power plants blocked the construction of a state plant in Seabrook, New Hampshire. In May 1977, two thousand protesters occupied the construction site and created a tent city on its premises, effectively shutting down building efforts. An organization called the Clamshell Alliance, a group based in Portsmouth, New Hampshire, took the lead in planning the takeover of the plant's construction site, including training protesters on how to carry out nonviolent resistance. The assault on the plant came from more than one direction, including some activists who arrived on boats that local lobster men commandeered. The fishermen supported the protestors because they believed that the nuclear power plant would wreak havoc on the lobster stocks in area waterways.[303]

Bob recalled, "Oh yeah, we had a big kitchen there," which was similar to the Rainbow Gatherings and OWS, with food and labor donated to sustain the movement.[304] New Hampshire officials conducted a raid on the occupation, arresting some 1,400 protesters, whom they charged with criminal trespassing. The protesters refused to post the required $500 bail and instead chose to serve out their two-week jail sentence. This strategy cost New Hampshire taxpayers an estimated $50,000 for the care of the incarcerated. The protesters also planned to return the following year with some 18,000 supporters unless plans to build the plant stopped.[305]

RAINBOW GATHERINGS

Hearing about the Rainbow Gatherings and its movement from Bob led me to want to find out more about it. I talked to a protester named Katie, who confirmed that the People's Kitchen evolved out of her experience at Rainbow Gatherings.

From Queens Village, New York, protester Katie worked as a substitute paraprofessional until the first day of the occupation of the park on September 17, when, she said, "I came down here and I stopped going there." Her previous experience as a waitress for six years and natural gravitation toward service had often resulted in her working in and around a kitchen. "My life did seem like it was naturally trending here, because for the past two years I've been traveling, visiting communities, communes, going to Rainbow Gatherings," she explained. "The way I set up the kitchen and a lot of the stuff I've contributed has led directly or was modified from Rainbow Gathering. What you see here is the child of protest and Rainbow Gatherings. Someone coined the term 'protestival' because it's a combination of 'protest' and 'festival.'"[306]

When I asked Katie what role she saw food playing in a social movement, she said, "I'm going to address directly the Rainbow experience for the moment because that's where my teaching and my learning is from. It was everything for me because you go there and you learn about giving and about service. One way to plug in, a way to be a part of the community there, is to plug into one of the kitchens." The Rainbow Gatherings exposes people to a "culture of service based around the food. The food is free and the community comes together and prepares it. Usually there is a group circle and one of the camps will serve the food. So it's about family, it's about togetherness, and it's about self and service." National Rainbow Gatherings attract "tens of thousands" of people, and "it could be more." Regionals often have "a hundred to a thousand." Each of the gatherings consists of different kitchen working groups. Each group has a distinct culture, cuisine and ideology that guides it.[307]

I learned that Rainbow Gatherings began around July 4, 1972, in the mountains of Colorado as a retreat for exhausted and mourning left-of-center activists and supporters of the U.S. peace movement. They had been convalescing in the forest after U.S. National Guard members killed four antiwar demonstrators at Kent State University in Ohio and two at Jackson State University in Mississippi. The first gathering also happened after U.S. president Richard Nixon ordered American forces to invade Cambodia. Those who attended the first gathering formed work groups to provide food and other basic necessities while camping. The first gathering lasted about three days. They focused on providing spiritual renewal for large groups of people disillusioned with the direction the country was headed in using rituals at the gatherings that were rooted in Native American spirituality.

The events attracted alternative groups of all stripes who, after the 1972 campout in state and federal parks, continued on an annual and semiannual basis under the umbrella of Rainbow Gathering.[308]

The first gathering attracted thousands of participants, resulting in the decision to organize similar events in the future. Thereafter, the dissidents organized national and regional Rainbow events. Free food prepared that emerged out of donations and distributed by members of a central kitchen twice a day has remained an original Rainbow idea and structure. The traditions around the central kitchen and the distribution of its food served as an important element of creating a sense of solidarity among Rainbow disciplines. These include a pre-meal food circle, holding hands within the circle, singing and repeating chants.[309]

I asked Katie what different things were done at the People's Kitchen compared to Rainbow Gatherings. She replied, "In contrast to the forest, here we purchase food and beverages from stores and we receive donations for food and resources from people and organizations; we don't have that luxury in the woods. The first few days were very, very rough. Organization was an issue. We kept getting all this dumpster bread, and there was an issue/concern about the health inspector. I ended up staying up all night organizing" the kitchen, which included making signage. "One of the signs that is very much like the Rainbow idea was 'If you see something that needs to be done, do it.'" That's an example of a Rainbow gathering philosophy that has shaped what's behind the People's Kitchen movement. That sign has empowered people to act and "gained us a lot of volunteers," said Katie. We have "a core group of at least twenty people in the kitchen right now that are empowered to act and don't feel like anyone's leading them and they work together. And hopefully that will grow because even now we're overworked."[310]

I asked Katie if she was the brains of the operation, and she said, "I would say I gave birth to it but at this point I'm just as much a player as anyone else." The People's Kitchen "has become its own organism and it [has] a life of its own….What happened was the first day I came here they put me to work. One of the working groups was food. I said, 'No, I'm not going to do the food bank.' But what I learned at Rainbow Gathering was… that in order to be part of the community, you have to work and you have to give of yourself in order to get back."[311]

AFTERWORD

THE PEOPLE'S KITCHEN

Katie recalled asking someone who had been charge of the kitchen

> *if I could help him make peanut butter and jelly sandwiches, and he said, "Of course." So I helped him for an hour or two and then walked away. Like a lot of people, he wasn't getting any sleep. He lives in the area. He said, "I need to go home and sleep. I trust you. Will you watch the kitchen?" I said OK and…basically from there I ended up taking on a leadership role. The next night was probably the night that I was up twenty-four hours cleaning the kitchen. It was all me and I was supposed to know everything.*[312]

I asked Katie if it was true that the People's Kitchen was literally getting pizzas sent from everywhere. "One of our members decided to send a message via Twitter asking people to send pizzas," she said. "That's when business at Liberatos Pizza started to really pick up." Activists in Wisconsin and Tahir Square employed this strategy to obtain donated pizza first.

To keep from getting burned out with all the hours she was giving to OWS, Katie said, "Right now, I'm setting up a program where I'm

People's Kitchen prep station. *Courtesy of Food Prof Photos.*

People's Kitchen volunteers make salad. *Courtesy of Food Prof Photos.*

bringing in teachers and leaders to help us sustain the kitchen. So, we'll see. We're learning."[313]

Randy, who made his way to OWS after hiking on the Appalachian Trail, was one of the most interesting people I came across at the People's Kitchen. I asked him how long he had been there, and he replied, "Just about a week. I was hiking on the Appalachian Trail, and every time I went out to resupply, I heard on the radio that the police had arrested 700 protestors who mobilized and blocked traffic on the Brooklyn Bridge. I had to support the movement. I also supported the civil rights movement, Vietnam War protest movement and the antinuke movement. I grew up during all of those. So, all those movements were my movements."[314] Randy provided an interesting context to how people were finding out about Occupy Wall Street and those who came from a long history of civil disobedience and protest.

Next, I met Joan, who came to Occupy Wall Street via San Francisco. She helped provide a sense of how a similar movement was going on the West Coast. "When we first started in San Francisco, we had a kitchen tent which had a stove. We were cooking on-site. The police came in and told us we had to take down the tent. There was a raid a few weeks ago that I was at on a Wednesday night where…seventy-five police officers in riot gear demolished the kitchen and dumped a lot of our possessions. So we lost a lot of food and we had to start just telling people to bring prepared food."[315]

I asked Joan what role she saw food playing in a movement like OWS, and she answered, "Food is a big part of it because" when people are making a movement a full-time job "it's vital to have food available." The fact that people are "stepping up…bringing food every single day, people who maybe are working people and can't camp out every night or they're older or have children, they're making an important contribution to the movement." Food, Joan says, is "just as vital as money contributions because even when you get money contributions there's all kinds of logistical issues that come into play when you have a non-hierarchical direct democracy system" like the one the OWS movement in "San Francisco and here are using....Who's in charge of the money? How do you access the money? What are the rules regarding the money? Bringing food is probably actually an even more direct way to help the movement, I think."[316] For instance, in the last week of October 2011, the Occupy Wall Street finance committee reported that it had spent $22,000 for food, medical care and laundry.[317]

Charlie came to Occupy Wall Street from Wisconsin, which had been embroiled in its conflict as Governor Scott Walker faced off against organized labor. He told me he had been at OWS for about three weeks. I asked where most of the food came from, and he replied, "It's mostly donations. Actually a really big contributor happens to be the Correctional Officers Union. We also get [some generous] donations from some churches." The Corrections Union gave OWS "$500 a week in Costco cards," and they provided transportation to Costco. "They make sure if we need supplies—because we get mostly food, obviously—but we need plates, napkins, gloves, you know, things like that, supplies that we need that aren't food, that we can go and get them at Costco."[318]

He shared with me a little bit about the running of the kitchen. "We serve food in three shifts: breakfast seven to noon, lunch noon to five, and dinner five to seven. We try to do a hard close at eleven, but most of the time, we still have a bunch of granola bars, stuff like that, that we just kind of put out and let people take themselves after we close. We do have off-site cooking. There's a place in East New York. We also have a place in Brooklyn where we go to cook off-site." Breakfast is catered.[319]

I met another woman, named Margaret, who was participating in her first social movement. "I guess you could say I've been sheltered," she told me.

I've been political but never to the extent like this. I read stories in the news about people saying they had to choose between going to the doctor or putting food on the table or paying their mortgage or feeding their kids; they had to make choices [about basic necessities] *that every human should have. One thing that gets my goat is knowing that 2,000 calories worth of junk food is cheaper than 2,000 calories worth of healthy food. And how many inner city people can't afford healthy food. And because of that, they're overweight. Hearing statistics like that moved me to take action. Our society must change for the better. So I joined OWS on September 30.*

AFTERWORD

She told me she had answered e-mails of support sent to the People's
Kitchen in which she noted, "A lot of people have been quoting Napoleon,
saying that the army marched on its stomach. That's been motivating them
to give us more food donations."[320]

WHERE ARE THE BLACK FOLKS?

After spending a few days in the park observing and talking with dozens of
people, I began to wonder: Is this a middle-class, white millennial movement?
In contrast to the recent Black Lives Matter movement, OWS looks more like
a Rainbow Gathering. I wanted to check my observations with other African
Americans at the park. I saw fewer than thirty black folks of the hundreds of
people who passed near the tables of People's Kitchen to get free food during
my two five-plus-hour days spent doing interviews in the park.

Earl was a single, African American man in his early twenties who was
born and raised in Brooklyn, New York. He explained to me why I didn't find
more black folks among the protestors. "It's sad to say, but our communities
are swallowing mainstream media's misrepresentation of the movement's
participants as spoiled, rich white kids and therefore are not identifying with
the protestors," he said. "I listen to Reverend Al Sharpton's *Hour of Power*
on Sunday nights on 98.7 KISS FM. Sharpton has been talking about the
respect that these kids should have for holding on so long" and encouraging
black folks to support and join the movement. "I respect Sharpton because
he gets involved. You can't say something isn't good if you don't go check
it out. And that's what I did when I came here." He went on to say, we,
as black folks, "should be supporting this movement 100 percent! We all
know someone in our community who is unemployed, dealing with bad
public schools, or needs affordable healthcare." An additional issue is ending
the current state of policing and the mass incarceration in this country of
disproportionally high numbers of poor black and brown people. Earl
concluded, "Black people should be here in full force just like the rest of the
world. But in my neighborhood, there's fear associated with protesting and
plenty of misinformation about the OWS movement."[321]

On my last day doing interviews, I noticed an African American male
in his mid-fifties observing the protesters from the edges of the park. He
looked like he was trying to understand what the movement stood for. With
so few blacks in the park, I wanted to know his thoughts about OWS and

People's Kitchen PB&J sandwiches. *Courtesy of Food Prof Photos.*

People's Kitchen volunteers prepare for the lunchtime meal. *Courtesy of Food Prof Photos.*

The serving table at People's Kitchen. *Courtesy of Food Prof Photos.*

its relevance for him, so I approached him and struck up a conversation. He told me he had been observing me as well, trying to understand my relationship to OWS. He told me his name was Malik and that he lived in Bed-Stuy, Brooklyn. "I'm looking at who's coming down here and I was shocked when I [saw actor] Alec Baldwin. I stood [on the side of the park] and just observed."[322]

I asked him the same questions I asked others, like what role does he think food plays in a social movement. "You have to have it, and it's something I want to do. I am homeless right now and I need a job. What I really want to do on a full-time basis, if God blesses me, is to feed some children seven days a week." Malik explained that feeding them is a way of letting them know "somebody cares about them....When you feed them then you can talk some sense into them....That's what activists did with Operation Breadbasket back in the day, brother."[323]

Operation Breadbasket started as an initiative of the SCLC in 1962. By 1966, the SCLC's Jesse Jackson took the initiative north to Chicago and other northern cities. In 1971, Jackson broke away from the SCLC in a dispute and went on to form Operation PUSH (People United to Save Humanity) in Chicago. PUSH members would go on to organize a number of initiatives, such as feeding the hungry to improve conditions in poor urban neighborhoods.

Similar to the efforts discussed in the Don't Buy Where You Can't Work Movements, in Chapter 1, PUSH organized boycotts against businesses who discriminated against blacks in their hiring and promotion practices.[324]

"When you give tough brothers good food, you can [sit down] with them and get some deep intel [about] what's troubling them and they won't rob you during the process," said Malik as he laughed. "So, I like what I've observed here with the People's Kitchen and all. This is a good movement."[325]

CONCLUSION

I met a young man from Orlando, Florida, named Justin who was a member of the People's Kitchen and was chronicling their work. He had been at OWS for a little more than twenty days and said he was working on a manual, a handbook of what OWS was doing that people could "adapt to their own cities and protest," he said. "We're going to create a PDF and hard copies [and distribute them]." The opening chapter of the book is entitled "The Importance of Food in Social Movements." Justin read a couple of lines from his work in progress:

> *Food is a right, not a privilege. Free food and access and empowerment toward sustainable movements in communities is the heart of the changes needed for an increasingly populated planet and its people. Food is freedom as sustainability empowers the people of this earth to be rid of any force that would seek to enslave, control, or intimidate them into a life of poverty so that a small few can grow fat off of the blood of innocent hardworking people.*[326]

I asked him what challenges the members of his working group had encountered while trying to feed this revolution. "It's hard to keep all the working parts organized and the food part of this movement is vital. [A body] can't last without a heart. The food is the heart." One of the chapters he had been working on emphasized the importance of love and food in this movement. Justin read from his manuscript: "The love that goes into the food is shared by the people who serve the food by the way they treat the people. It makes the food better. It makes the food healthier. It makes the person who's eating it feel better…and want to [support the movement]." Another problem he told me about was that "it's real hard to prepare on-site" and comply with local "health codes. That's one of the things we're going to address in the book, the importance of abiding by local health codes so that the police have a hard time shutting [a movement's kitchen] down."[327]

Justin concluded, "In two weeks, we've gained so much knowledge and so much experience doing this. A day feels like a year. I really want to be able to share a document that can…empower people to start their own food committees, to start their own sustainability groups, [and] help movements like this one."[328]

New York Times columnist Mark Bittman had this to say about the OWS movement: "What we need are more activists who are interested in food than 'food activists.'" OWS, which had the support of organized labor and other progressive organizations, represented an old strategy for forcing fundamental change. It served as part of a U.S. tradition dating back to "the populist, suffragist, labor, civil rights, women's, anti-war, environmental, and even food movements." Bittman observed that "energy, frustration, anger, perception, pizza, and apples paid for by supporters or donated by farmers and, ultimately, by its daily growth" sustained the movement, which he describes as one "that questions everything—from food justice to economic justice."[329]

As I have shown in this book, history provides evidence that revolutionary protests are required to bring about progressive change. And change begins when protestors make the public aware of the issues that are negatively affecting their lives. The food-related issues have changed over the decades, but direct-action protest continues to be an effective method to pressure elected officials to act for the greater good. This book suggests a proven strategy for private citizens today to address important food-related issues, such as the need for equal access to nutritious food and clean water and repairing our country's broken food system. It also provides a movement template for addressing concerns that OWS activists raised in 2011—the need for affordable healthcare and housing and to address global warming and end corporate control of public elections.

NOTES

INTRODUCTION

1. For more on when the concentration of African Americans shifted away from the South see, Isabel Wilkerson, *The Warmth of Others Suns: The Epic Story of the Great Migration* (New York: Random House, 2010).

CHAPTER 1

2. Frederick Douglass Opie interview with Fred Opie Jr., summer 2005.
3. *Call & Post*, September 7, 1940.
4. Christopher Robert Reed, *The Rise of Chicagos Black Metropolis, 1920–1929* (Urbana: University of Illinois Press, 2011), 141.
5. Ibid., 1, 67–69, 74, 76, 141, 147.
6. *New Journal & Guide*, October 7, 1933; *New York Times*, August 28, 1938; *New Negro Alliance v. Sanitary Grocery Co.*, FindLaw.com, http://caselaw.lp.findlaw.com/scripts/getcase.pl?court=US&vol=303&invol=552.
7. Christopher Robert Reed, *The Depression Comes to the South Side: Protest and Politics in the Black Metropolis, 1930–1933* (Bloomington: Indiana University Press, 2011), 67–68.
8. Ibid., 67.
9. Ibid., 68–69, 74, 76.
10. *New Journal & Guide*, October 7, 1933; *New York Times*, August 28, 1938; *Call & Post*, September 7, 1940.
11. *New Journal & Guide*, December 23, 1933; *Washington Post*, September 3, 1933.
12. *Chicago Daily Tribune*, May 18, 1933.

13. *Pittsburgh Courier*, March 4, 1933.
14. *New Journal & Guide*, April 29, 1933.
15. *Philadelphia Tribune*, July 13, 1933.
16. *Afro-American*, July 15, 1933.
17. Ibid.
18. *Pittsburgh Courier*, December 30, 1933.
19. *Chicago Daily Tribune*, May 18, 1933.
20. *Chicago Defender*, October 7, 1933; *Afro-American*, January 6, 1934.
21. *Chicago Defender*, September 30, 1933.
22. Ibid.; quoted from *Washington Post*, September 3, 1933.
23. Hayward Farrar, *The Baltimore* Afro-American, *1892–1950* (Greenwood Publishing Group, 1998), 135–36.
24. *Afro-American*, October 7, 1933.
25. The two restaurants in Harlem are mentioned in *The Marcus Garvey and Universal Negro Improvement Association Papers*, vol. 7, edited by Robert A. Hill (University of California Press, 1983), 982–83. Garvey's Negro Factories Corporation (NFC), which in the early 1920s had among its many enterprises three grocery stores and two restaurants in Harlem, is discussed in Frederick Douglass Opie, *Black Labor Migration in Caribbean Guatemala, 1882–1923*, Florida Work in the Americas Series (Gainsville: University of Florida Press, 2009), 92.
26. *Afro-American*, November 5, 1932.
27. Ibid.; October 7, 1933; November 8, 1941; October 14, 1933.
28. Ibid., October 7, 1933; November 8, 1941.
29. *Chicago Defender*, September 30, 1933; *New Journal & Guide*, October 14, 1933, and December 30, 1933; *Afro-American*, October 14, 1933, and January 6, 1934.
30. *Pittsburgh Courier*, January 27, 1934.
31. *Washington Post*, September 3, 1933; *Chicago Defender*, September 30, 1933; *New Journal & Guide*, December 2, 1933; *Pittsburgh Courier*, December 9, 1933; *Afro-American*, July 21, 1934.
32. *New Journal & Guide*, December 23, 1933.
33. *Chicago Defender*, September 30, 1933; *New York Amsterdam News*, October 4, 1933; *Afro-American*, July 21, 1934.
34. *Afro-American*, September 16, 1933.
35. *New Journal & Guide*, September 30, 1933.
36. *Afro-American*, October 7, 1933.
37. *New Journal & Guide*, June 4, 1938.
38. Ibid., September 30, 1933; *Afro-American*, November 4, 1933.
39. *New Journal & Guide*, October 7, 1933.
40. Ibid.
41. *New Journal & Guide*, October 7, 1933; October 14, 1933; *Afro-American* October 21, 1933.

42. *Afro-American*, October 7, 1933.

43. *Pittsburgh Courier*, November 18, 1933.

44. *New Journal & Guide*, October 7, 1933; *Call & Post*, October 15, 1936.

45. *Pittsburgh Courier*, December 2, 1933; *New Journal & Guide*, December 23, 1933.

46. *Afro-American*, December 16, 1933.

47. *Pittsburgh Courier*, December 9, 1933.

48. *New Journal & Guide*, December 23, 1933.

49. *Pittsburgh Courier*, December 9, 1933.

50. *New Journal & Guide*, August 11, 1934.

51. *Pittsburgh Courier*, December 30, 1933.

52. *Afro-American*, January 6, 1934.

53. Ibid., January 27, 1934.

54. *Pittsburgh Courier*, January 27, 1934.

55. Ibid.

56. *Chicago Defender*, April 18, 1936.

57. Ibid.

58. *New York Amsterdam News*, December 21, 1938; *Cleveland Call & Post*, September 7, 1940.

59. *Cleveland Call & Post*, September 7, 1940.

60. *Call & Post*, September 7, 1940.

61. Ibid.

62. *New York Amsterdam News*, December 21, 1938.

63. Ibid.

64. *Call & Post*, August 18, 1938.

65. *New York Amsterdam News*, December 16, 1939.

66. Adam Clayton Powell Jr., *Adam by Adam: The Autobiography of Adam Clayton Powell, Jr.* (New York: Dial Press, 1971), 62–63.

67. *Call & Post*, September 7, 1940.

68. Powell, *Adam by Adam*, 64.

69. *New York Amsterdam News*, November 23, 1940.

70. Ibid., August 13, 1930.

71. *Afro-American*, May 3, 1941.

CHAPTER 2

72. *Chicago Defender*, October 2, 1943.

73. Julie L. McGee, *David C. Driskell: Artist and Scholar* (San Francisco: Pomegranate, 2006), 13.

74. David C. Driskell, interview with the author, 2011.

75. *New Journal & Guide*, December 18, 1937.

76. Ibid.

77. *New York Amsterdam Star-News*, October 24, 1942; *Chicago Defender*, October 2, 1943.

78. *New York Amsterdam Star-News*, October 24, 1942.

79. *Pittsburgh Courier*, September 28, 1940.

80. *New York Amsterdam News*, January 13, 1945.

81. *Washington Post*, July 2, 1952.

82. *Washington Post, Times Herald*, September 18, 1960.

83. Driskell, interview.

84. Ibid.

85. Ibid.

86. Ibid.

87. *Washington Post*, December 11, 1948.

88. *Atlanta Daily World*, October 11, 1949.

89. Mary Eliza Church Terrell, *A Colored Woman in a White World* (Washington, D.C.: Ransdell Inc. Printers and Publishers, 1940), 385.

90. Ibid.

91. Jan Whitaker, "Early Chains: John R. Thompson," *Restaurant-ing Through History*, June 10, 2010, http://restaurant-ingthroughhistory. com/2010/06/10/early-chains-john-r-thompson.

92. *Chicago Defender*, January 31, 1953.

93. Ibid.

94. Powell, *Adam by Adam*, 82–83.

95. Ibid., 83.

96. Ibid., 97.

97. Ibid.

98. Ibid., 98.

99. For more on Little Rock, see Karen Anderson, *Little Rock: Race and Resistance at Central High School* (Princeton, NJ: Princeton University Press, 2013).

100. Powell, *Adam by Adam*, 16.

101. Rufus Estes, *Good Things to Eat, as Suggested by Rufus; A Collection of Practical Recipes for Preparing Meats, Game, Fowl, Fish, Puddings, Pastries, Etc.* (Chicago: Rufus Estes, 1911), 71, 81.

102. Powell, *Adam by Adam*, 17–18.

CHAPTER 3

103. Fred D. Gray, *Bus Ride to Justice: Changing the System by the System; The Life and Works of Fred D. Gray, Preacher, Attorney, Politician* (Montgomery, AL: New South Books, 2002), 36–38.

104. Ibid., 52–54; Aldon D. Morris, *The Origins of the Civil Rights Movement* (New York: Free Press, 1984), 43–44.

105. Jo Ann Gibson Robinson, ed., with a foreword by David J. Garrow, *The Montgomery Bus Boycott and the Women Who Started It: The Memoir of Jo Ann Gibson Robinson* (Knoxville: University of Tennessee Press, 1987), 71.

106. Interview with Georgia Gilmore, conducted by Blackside Inc. for the documentary *Eyes on the Prize: America's Civil Rights Years (1954–1965)*, February 17, 1986, Washington University Libraries, Film and Media Archive, Henry Hampton Collection; "Role of Georgia Gilmore and Her Southern Cooking in the Civil Rights Movement," *Morning Edition*, National Public Radio, March 4, 2005.

107. Interview with Georgia Gilmore.

108. Ibid.

109. Ibid.

110. Ibid.

111. *Washington Post*, July 24, 1989.

112. Ibid.

113. *Baltimore Afro-American*, December 9, 1939.

114. *Washington Post*, July 24, 1989.

115. Ibid.

116. "Role of Georgia Gilmore."

117. *Washington Post*, July 24, 1989.

CHAPTER 4

118. Leon Fink and Brian Greenberg, *Upheaval in the Quiet Zone: A History of Hospital Workers' Union, Local 1199* (Urbana: University of Illinois Press, 1989), 1.

119. Fink and Greenberg, *Upheaval in the Quiet Zone*, 30.

120. Ibid., 32.

121. Ken Downs, Montefiore Hospital interview transcripts, 1975, Kheel Center, Cornell University, Box 5680OH, 1, 14, Sub-Series X-D.

122. Ibid.

123. Ibid.

124. Ibid.

125. Ibid.

126. Ibid.

127. Ibid.

128. Ibid.

129. Ibid.

130. Karen Hess, *The Carolina Rice Kitchen: The African Connection* (Columbia: University of South Carolina Press, 1992), 96.

131. Thelma Bowles, Montefiore Hospital interview transcripts, Kheel Center, Cornell University, Box 5680OH, 1, 5, Sub-Series X-D.

132. Ibid.

133. Ibid.

134. Officials and Executive Board of Local 585 to Members, May 13, 1959, Kheel Center, Cornell University, Collection 5510, Box 46, Folder Contributions Food.

135. Fink and Greenberg, *Upheaval in the Quiet Zone*, 77, 79.

136. Bowles, Montefiore Hospital interview transcripts.

137. Ted Mitchell interview, 2 transcript, 1976, Kheel Center, Cornell University, Box 5680OH, 1, 44, Sub-Sub-Sub-Series X-A-1-I.

138. *1199 News*, December 1999.

139. A. Philip Randolph to Friends, June 22, 1962, Kheel Center, Cornell University, Collection 5510, Box 46, Folder Messages From Unions, Org, Ind. Re Strike.

140. Bayard Rustin, interview transcript, 1977, Kheel Center, Cornell University, Box 56900H, 2, 56, Sub-Sub-Series X-F-4, 15.

141. Ibid.

142. *New York Times*, November 19, 2005; James Jennings and Monte Rivera, *Puerto Rican Politics in Urban America* (Washington, D.C.: University Press of America, 1977), 44–46.

143. William K. De Fossett, report on the Emergency Action Convention on June 29, 1962, in the office of A. Phillip Randolph, Bureau of Special Services, July 2, 1962, Kheel Center, Cornell University, Box 6140, 3, 38, Malcolm X File, 1-3; Joseph Monserrat and A. Philip Randolph to Friends of the Committee, July 30, 1962, Kheel Center, Cornell University, Collection 5510, Box 48 Strike—Ten Hospitals—May, 1960, Folder Committee for Justice to Hospital Workers & Prayer Pilgrimage July 22, 1962; *New York Times*, September 1, 1995; July 20, 2006.

144. *1199 News*, Winter 1993.

145. De Fossett, report on the Emergency Action Convention.

146. Ibid.

147. Ibid.

148. Ibid.

149. Ibid.

150. Ibid.

151. Ibid.

152. Moe Foner with Dan North, foreword by Ossie Davis, *Not for Bread Alone: A Memoir* (Ithaca: Cornell University Press, 2002), 60.

153. Committee for Justice to Hospital Workers, Prayer Pilgrimage Flyer, "Join the PRAYER PILGRAMGE In Support of the Hospital Strikers," circa July 15 and July 21, 1962, Kheel Center, Cornell University, Collection 5510,

Box 48 Strike—Ten Hospitals—May, 1960, Folder Committee for Justice to Hospital Workers & Prayer Pilgrimage, July 22, 1962.

154. *1199 News*, Winter 1993.

155. Dr. Martin Luther King Jr. Address to Prayer Pilgrimage, July 22, 1962, Kheel Center, Cornell University, Collection 5510, Box 48 Strike—Ten Hospitals—May 1960, Folder Committee for Justice to Hospital Workers & Prayer Pilgrimage, July 22, 1962.

156. Ibid., 1–2.

157. Monserrat and Randolph to Friends of the Committee.

158. Fink and Greenberg, *Upheaval in the Quiet Zone*, 113.

159. Resolutions Adopted by the Committee for Justice to Hospital Workers, July 21, 1962, Kheel Center, Cornell University, Collection 5510, Box 48 Strike—Ten Hospitals—May 1960, Folder Committee for Justice to Hospital Workers & Prayer Pilgrimage, July 22, 1962.

160. Ibid.

CHAPTER 5

161. Leah Chase, interview with April Grayson, 2004, Southern Foodways Alliance Founders Project.

162. Ibid.

163. *Cleveland Call & Post*, December 13, 1941.

164. *Pittsburgh Courier*, September 23, 1944; *Afro-American*, August 21, 1948.

165. *Pittsburgh Courier*, November 18, 1944.

166. *Gourmet*, February 2000.

167. *Pittsburgh Courier*, December 25, 1954.

168. Chase, interview.

169. *Chicago Defender*, July 14, 1951.

170. Chase, interview.

171. Raphael Cassimere Jr., interview with Grant Werner, Kate Welton, Emma Whitman and Hannah Welsh, 2012, *The Nation's Longest Struggle: Looking Back on the Modern Civil Rights Movement*, D.C. Everest Oral History Project, http://www.dceoralhistoryproject.org.

172. Ibid.

173. Ibid.

174. *Chicago Defender*, September 24, 1960.

175. *Afro-American*, October 1, 1960.

176. *New York Amsterdam News*, October 28, 1961.

177. *Cleveland Call & Post*, November 4, 1961; *Afro-American*, December 30, 1961; November 9, 1963.

178. *Chicago Daily Defender*, October 29, 1963.

179. Ibid.
180. Ibid., November 6, 1963; *Afro-American*, November 9, 1963.
181. Chase, interview.
182. *Pittsburgh Courier*, February 20, 1965.
183. "Dooky Chase's Restaurant," Citysearch, http://neworleans.citysearch. com/profile/4432184/new_orleans_la/dooky_chase_restaurant.html.
184. Ibid.
185. Cassimere, interview.
186. James Vaughn Paschal and Mae Armster Kendall, *Paschal: Living the Dream* (Lincoln, NE: iUniverse, 2006), 124–26, 228.
187. Marcellas C.D. Barksdale, interview with the author, 2005.
188. *Atlanta Daily World*, June 30, 1934.
189. Bob Jeffries, *Soul Food Cook Book* (Indianapolis: Bobbs-Merril Company, 1969), vii.
190. *Chicago Daily Defender*, February 22, 1968.
191. Ibid., February 12, 1968.
192. Paschal and Kendall, *Paschal*, 127.
193. Ibid.
194. *Chicago Daily Defender*, December 12, 1967.
195. Betty Joyce Johnson, interview with the author, 2005.
196. Lonnie King, interview by Bob Short, September 2009, "Reflections on Georgia Politics," ROGP-086, Lonnie King, Richard B. Russell Library for Political Research and Studies, University of Georgia, Athens.
197. Short, interview.
198. Ibid. For more on Mays, see Randal Maurice Jelks, *Benjamin Elijah Mays, Schoolmaster of the Movement: A Biography* (Chapel Hill: University of North Carolina Press, 2012).
199. King, interview.
200. Paschal and Kendall, *Paschal*, 26.
201. Ibid., 125.
202. *Chicago Defender*, December 31, 1966.
203. King, interview.
204. Paschal and Kendall, *Paschal*, 125–27.
205. Ibid., 127.
206. King, interview.
207. Ibid.
208. Ibid.
209. Paschal and Kendall, *Paschal*, 126.
210. King, interview.; for more on Kennedy's involvement in King's negotiated release from jail in Atlanta and the implication for the 1960 presidential election, see Larry Tye, *Bobby Kennedy: The Making of a Liberal Icon* (New York: Random House, 2016).

211. King, interview.

212. Ibid.

213. Joe York, *Smokes and Ears*, Southern Foodways Alliance Documentary Film, http://www.southernfoodways.org/film/smokes-ears.

214. Ibid.

215. Ibid.

216. Ibid.

217. Ibid.

CHAPTER 6

218. The Educational Radio Network's (hereafter ERN) coverage of the March on Washington for Jobs and Freedom, eight of fifteen hours of broadcast: 3:56 p.m.–4:25 p.m., August 28, 1963, WGBH Media Library & Archives.

219. Ibid.

220. Ibid.

221. Thomas Gentile, *March on Washington: August 28, 1963* (Washington, D.C.: New Day Publications, 1983), 1, 47, 94.

222. John F. Kennedy, "Radio and Television Address on Civil Rights, June 11, 1963," *Papers of John F. Kennedy, President's Office Files,* JFKPOF-045-005, 3, John F. Kennedy Public Library and Museum Archives.

223. Harry Belafonte, *My Song: A Memoir* (New York: Knopf, 2011), 278.

224. Ibid.

225. Gentile, *March on Washington*, 1.

226. Ibid., 4–6.

227. Frederick Douglass Opie, *Upsetting the Apple Cart: Black and Latino Coalitions in New York City from Protest to Public Office*, Columbia History of Urban Life Series, edited by Kenneth Jackson (New York: Columbia University Press, 2014), 41–48.

228. Rustin, interview transcript.

229. Gentile, *March on Washington*, 3–4.

230. Ibid., 4.

231. *Chicago Defender,* August 17, 1963.

232. Cleveland Robinson and Bayard Rustin, *March on Washington Organizing Manual* (N.p.: Deklare Printing, 1963), 10.

233. Joyce White, *Soul Food: Recipes and Reflections from African-American Churches* (New York: Harper and Collins, 1998), 1–2.

234. *New York Amsterdam News*, August 17, 1963.

235. Ibid.

236. ERN, 10:00 a.m.–11:00 a.m., August 28, 1963.

237. Ibid.; *Chicago Defender*, August 17, 1963.
238. James Weldon Johnson, *Along This Way: The Autobiography of James Weldon Johnson* (New York: Viking Press, 1933), 64.
239. Bennett Singer, Nancy Kates, Walter Naegel and Hasan Jeffries, "The Life of Civil Rights Pioneer Bayard Rustin," *All Sides with Ann Fisher*, WOSU Public Radio, February 18, 2013, http://radio.wosu.org/post/life-civil-rights-pioneer-bayard-rustin.
240. Hilary Parkinson, "The March," U.S. National Archives Blog, August 26, 2011, http://blogs.archives.gov/prologue/?p=6691.
241. *Pittsburgh Courier*, August 31, 1963.
242. Ibid.
243. Ibid.; *Chicago Defender*, August 17, 1963.
244. *Chicago Defender*, August 17, 1963; *Pittsburgh Courier*, August 31, 1963.
245. *New York Times*, August 27, 1963.
246. Carol Ardman, first-person account of the March on Washington, August 2013.
247. Nancy Schimmel, first-person account of the March on Washington, August 2013, http://peoplesworld.org/three-days-on-bus-then-dancing-at-march-on-washington.
248. Ibid.; *New York Times*, August 27, 1963.
249. *New York Times*, August 28, 1963.
250. Schimmel, first-person account; Gentile, *March on Washington*, 203.
251. Frederick Douglass Opie, *Hog and Hominy: Soul Food from Africa to America* (New York: Columbia University Press, 2008), 5–12, 33–40; Frederick Douglass Opie, *Zora Neale Hurston on Florida Food: Recipes, Remedies and Simple Pleasures* (Charleston, SC: The History Press, 2015), 81–84.
252. Jualynne E. Dodson and Cheryl Townsend Gilkes, "There's Nothing like Church Food: Food and the U.S. Afro-Christian Tradition: Re-Membering Community and Feeding the Embodied S/spirit(s)," *Journal of the American Academy of Religion* 63, no. 3: 523.
253. ERN, 11:00 a.m.–12:00 a.m., August 28, 1963.
254. *Washington Post*, August 24, 2011,
255. *Afro-American*, September 7, 1963; ERN, 11:58 a.m.–1:00 p.m., August 28, 1963.
256. Belafonte, *My Song: A Memoir*, 278.
257. *New York Times*, August 28, 1963.
258. Belafonte, *My Song: A Memoir*, 278.
259. Ibid.
260. ERN, 11:58 a.m.–1:00 p.m., August 28, 1963.
261. *Chicago Defender*, August 17, 1963.
262. Belafonte, *My Song: A Memoir*, 278.
263. ERN, 1:58:30 p.m., August 28, 1963.

CHAPTER 7

264. Malcolm X, with the assistance of Alex Haley, *The Autobiography of Malcolm X* (New York: Ballantine Books, 1964), 8.

265. *Washington Post*, May 17, 1960; December 11, 1960.

266. Ibid., May 17, 1960; *New York Amsterdam News*, September 3, 1960.

267. Malcolm X, *Autobiography*, 215–21.

268. *Washington Post*, December 11, 1960; *New York Times*, April 23, 1961.

269. *Washington Post*, May 17, 1960; C. Eric Lincoln, *The Black Muslims in America*, 3rd ed. (Grand Rapids, MI: Wm. B. Eerdmans Publishing Co., 1994), 18.

270. Lincoln, *Black Muslims in America*, 18.

271. Ibid., 87–88.

272. Ibid.

273. Ibid.

274. *Muhammad Speaks*, March 15, 1968.

275. Ibid; *New York Times*, April 23, 1961.

276. Martha Frances Lee, *The Nation of Islam: An American Millenarian Movement* (Syracuse, NY: Syracuse University Press, 1996), 41; *Philadelphia Tribune*, April 18, 1964.

277. *Muhammad Speaks*, March 15, 1968.

278. *Washington Post*, December 11, 1960.

279. *Muhammad Speaks*, March 15, 1968.

280. Ibid.

281. Lincoln, *Black Muslims*, 89.

282. *Muhammad Speaks*, March 15, 1968.

283. Ibid.

284. Ibid.

285. Lincoln, *Black Muslims in America*, 88; *Washington Post*, December 11, 1960.

286. *Wall Street Journal*, May 16, 1963.

287. Rudy Bradshaw, interview with author, summer 2005; Eugene Watts, interview with the author, summer 2005.

288. Unlike the pie at Restaurant Shabazz, this "whirlwind version that stars a can of Boston baked beans" would not be used by Orthodox Muslims. Boston baked beans are prepared with salt pork, which is forbidden to them.

289. Watts, interview.

AFTERWORD

290. "Occupy Wall Street: From a Blog Post to a Movement," *Around the Nation*, NPR, October 20, 2011, http://www.npr.org/2011/10/20/141530025/occupy-wall-street-from-a-blog-post-to-a-movement.

291. Ibid.; *Ottawa Citizen*, November 3, 2011; Daniel Levitsky-Lang and Amy Lang, eds., *Dreaming in Public: The Building of the Occupy Movement* (Oxford, UK: New Internationalist, 2012), 30.

292. *New York Times*, October 11, 2011; Marina Sitrin, "Horizontalism: From Argentina to Wall Street," *NACLA Report on the Americas* 44 no. 6 (November/December 2011): 8–11.

293. Jean E. Jackson and Kay B. Warren, "Indigenous Movements in Latin America, 1992–2004: Controversies, Ironies, New Directions," *Annual Review of Anthropology* 34 (October 2005): 549–73; Aída Hernández R. Castillo, "Zapatismo and the Emergence of Indigenous Feminism," *NACLA Report on the Americas* 35 no. 6 (2002): 39; Sitrin, "Horizontalism." For more on the Zapatista movement, see Courtney Jung, *The Moral Force of Indigenous Politics: Critical Liberalism and the Zapatistas* (New York: Cambridge University Press, 2008).

294. Levitsky-Lang and Lang, *Dreaming in Public*, 300–302; Sitrin, "Horizontalism."

295. Levitsky-Lang and Lang, *Dreaming in Public*, 300–302.

296. *New York Times*, January 22, 2011.

297. Ibid.

298. *New York Times*, October 25, 2011.

299. Arun Gupta, *In These Times* 35, no 12 (December 2011): 18–20, 27.

300. *Sojourners* magazine, December 2011.

301. Bob, interview with the author, October 2011. The names of those interviewed have been changed for the safety of the participants.

302. Ibid.

303. *Time*, May 16, 1977.

304. Bob, interview.

305. *Time*, May 16, 1977.

306. Katie, interview with the author, October 2011.

307. Ibid.

308. Memoirs on the Rainbow Gathering website: http://www.welcomehome.org/rainbow/hipstory/roots.html; http://www.welcomehome.org/rainbow/hipstory/origin.html. [Note: This website worked at the time the author researched and wrote this section of the book. However, months later, it has not been functioning at the time of final book edits.]

309. Iddo Tavory and Yehuda C. Goodman, "A Collective of Individuals: Between Self and Solidarity in a Rainbow Gathering," *Sociology of Religion* 70, no. 3 (Fall 2009): 267–68, 271.

310. Katie, interview.

311. Ibid.

312. Ibid.

313. Ibid.

314. Randy interview by author, October 2011.
315. Joan interview by author, October 2011.
316. Ibid.
317. *Ottawa Citizen*, November 3, 2011.
318. Bob, interview.
319. Ibid.
320. Margaret interview by author, October 2011.
321. Earl interview by author, October 2011.
322. Malik interview by author, October 2011.
323. Ibid.
324. Opie, *Upsetting the Apple Cart*, 130, 145–46.
325. Malik, interview.
326. Justin interview by author, October 2011.
327. Ibid.
328. Ibid.
329. *New York Times*, October 11, 2011.

INDEX

A

AACS 18, 20
Adbusters 155
AFL 16, 34, 82, 83, 122
Afro-American Cooking School
    (AACS) 18
Alabama 37, 59, 60, 62, 63, 69, 107,
    108, 126, 151
Ali, Muhammad 154
American Federation of Labor (AFL) 16
American Jewish Congress 125
Anderson, Henry 28
A&P 20, 23, 25, 27, 28
Arsdale, Harry Van 80
Atlanta University Center (AUC) 99, 109

B

Baker, Josephine 140
Baldwin, James 84
Baltimore 15, 18, 20, 132
Belafonte, Harry 121, 136, 181
Beth-El Hospital 82, 83
Bibb, Joseph D. 10
Big Apple Inn 117
Bittman, Mark 156

Black Muslims in America, The 151
black newspapers 38
Blaikie, Miller, and Hines Inc. 129
Bohemian Cavern 47
Bond, Julian 108
Bouazizi, Mohamed 157
Bowles, Thelma 79
box lunches 127, 132
Bronzeville 9

C

Campaign for Nuclear Disarmament
    (CND) 162
Canal Street 90
Carver, George Washington 62
Cassimere, Raphael, Jr. 99
Catholic University 41
Chase, Dooky 89, 90, 91, 92, 97, 118
Chase, Leah 89
Chicago 10
Chitlin' Circuit 42
Clamshell Alliance 162
Clore's Guest House 44
Club from Nowhere 60
Colored Clerks Circle 34

INDEX

Committee for Justice to Hospital Workers (CJHW) 85
Committee on Appeal for Human Rights (COAHR) 109
Communist Party 34
Congress for Racial Equality (CORE) 83, 95, 97, 105, 123, 129, 149
Congress of Industrial Organizations (CIO) 34
Consumers' League of Greater New Orleans (CLGNO) 91
Coordinating Committee for Employment (CCE) 34
Coordinating Committee for the Enforcement of D.C. Anti-Discrimination Laws (CCEDA) 48
Correctional Officers Union 167

D

Davis, John Aubrey 17
Davis, Leon 82
Davis, Ossie 84
Department of Justice 40
Dexter Avenue Baptist Church 60
District 65 84
Dixiecrats 40
Double V campaign 90
Downs, Ken 72
Driskell, Dr. David C. 41
Dryades Street 90
Dull, Henrietta Stanley 103

E

Eisenhower, Dwight D. 52
1199 71, 72, 80, 81, 82, 83, 84, 85, 87, 177, 178, 179
entertainers 140
Evers, Medger 118

F

Fair Employment Practices Committee (FEPC) 120

Farish Street 117
Farmer, James 85
Farrakhan, Louis 143
Fauntroy, Walter 129
Federal Reserve Bank 40
Ferguson, Dutton 25
Fisher, Doris 18
Foner, Mo 80
Freemasons 20
fried chicken 132

G

Garvey, Marcus 16
Gilmore, Georgia 60
Godoff, Elliot 72
GOOD FOODS CORP 151
Government Services Incorporated (GSI) 138
Great Depression 10, 18, 20, 145
Greensboro, North Carolina 107, 110

H

Harlem 20, 34, 35, 37, 52, 72, 84, 85, 128, 138, 146, 153
Hastie, William H. 17, 26, 28, 32, 33, 39
High's Ice Cream Store Campaign 28
Hoover, J. Edgar 121
Horne, Lena 140
Howard Johnson's 132
Howard University 18, 23, 41

I

indignados 156

J

Jackson, Mahalia 140
Jackson State University 163
Jasmine Revolution 157
Jeffries, Bob 102, 180
Jim Crow 8
Johnson, James Weldon 127

K

Kennedy, John F. 99
Kent State University 163
King, Martin Luther, Jr. (MLK) 59, 60,
    61, 68, 105, 113, 116, 123, 179
Kroger 34

L

Lawson, Belford, Jr. 17
Lee, Gene 119
Lewis, James W. 17
Liberatos Pizza 165
Lincoln, C. Eric 148, 151, 183
Little Rock High School 53
Long, Carolyn 109
Louisiana Association for the Progress
    of Negro Citizens 91
Lunford Beer Garden and Restaurant 44

M

Malcolm X 84, 86, 87, 143, 146, 149,
    178, 183
Manhattan Eye, Ear and Throat
    Institute 82
March on Washington 8, 120
March on Washington Organizing Manual,
    The 125
Mays, Benjamin E. 108
McCrory's 95
Miller, Kelly 22
Mississippi Freedom Summer 105
Monserrat, Joseph 83
Montefiore 73
Montgomery Bus Boycott 59
Montgomery Improvement Association
    (MIA) 60
Mora, Juan "Big John" 117
Mount Sinai 82
Muhammad, Elijah 84, 145
Muhammad Speaks 148

N

Napoleon 7, 168
National Association for the
    Advancement of Colored People
    (NAACP) 10
National Catholic Conference 125
National Council of Churches of
    Christ 125
National Gallery of Art 47
National Recovery Administration
    (NRA) 15
Nation of Islam 8, 143
Negro Factories Corporation (NFC) 20
Newman, Paul 140
New Negro Alliance (NNA) 10, 15, 17,
    18, 22, 23, 33
New Orleans 89
New Orleans Ministerial Alliance 97
New Orleans Public Service Inc.
    (NOPS) 96
Nixon, E.D. 59
Nixon, Richard 99, 163

O

Occupy Wall Street 155
Operation Breadbasket 170

P

Paschal, James and Robert 99
Paschal's 99
People's Defense League (PDL) 90
People's Kitchen 155
People United to Save Humanity
    (PUSH) 170
Pierce, Joseph 109
Piggly Wiggly 25
Porter, James Hale 10
Powell, Adam Clayton, Jr. 35, 52,
    53, 175
protestival 163

INDEX

Q

"Queen of Creole Cuisine" 98

R

Rainbow Gatherings 162
Randolph, A. Philip 34, 59, 82, 122, 178
Riverside Church 128
Robinson, Cleveland 84, 85, 122, 181
Rockefeller, Nelson 85
Roosevelt, Franklin D. (FDR) 8, 15, 16, 22, 39, 90, 91, 122
Russell, Bertrand 162

S

Sanborns 47
Saverin Restaurant 47
Schuldt, Gus A. 26
Seabrook 162
Shabazz Restaurant 151
Sharpton, Al 168
Shaw neighborhood 42
sit-ins 107
Southern Christian Leadership Conference (SCLC) 105, 170
Stanley, W. Payne 26
Strand Ballroom 20
Student Nonviolent Coordinating Committee (SNCC) 113, 117, 123, 132, 149
Sullivan, Herschelle 108
Sutton, Percy 86

T

Tahir Square 165
Temple Luncheonette and Drug Company 23
Terrell, Mary Church 49
Thompson's Restaurant 49
Treme neighborhood 89

U

United Presbyterian Church 125
Urban League 9, 10, 16, 34, 83, 123

V

Valentín, Gilberto Gerena 84
Vietnam War 166

W

Walker, Cora 84
Walter Francis White 126
Ward, James 18, 25
Washington, Booker T. 16, 62
Washington, D.C. 10, 23, 40, 48, 153
Washington Restaurant Association (WRA) 52
Wilkins, Roy 86, 123
Williams, Ellis A. 35
Works Progress Administration (WPA) 74, 143
World Council of Churches 129

Y

YMCA 22

Z

Zapatista movement 156
Zoro Bread Company 82
Zuccotti Park 155

ABOUT THE AUTHOR

Frederick Douglass Opie is a professor of history and foodways at Babson College and the author of *Hog and Hominy: Soul Food from Africa to America*; *Black Labor Migration in Caribbean Guatemala, 1882–1923*; *Upsetting the Apple Cart: Black and Latino Coalitions in New York From Protest to Public Office*; and *Zora Neale Hurston on Florida Food: Recipes, Remedies and Simple Pleasures*. Opie is a regular contributor on the radio show *The Splendid Table*.

Visit us at
www.historypress.net
....
This title is also available as an e-book